ROYAL NAVY MEDITERRANEAN FLEET 1793–1805

The war at sea against Napoleon

Casey Baker
Illustrated by Edouard A. Groult

OSPREY PUBLISHING
Bloomsbury Publishing Plc
Kemp House, Chawley Park, Cumnor Hill, Oxford OX2 9PH, UK
Bloomsbury Publishing Ireland Limited,
29 Earlsfort Terrace, Dublin 2, D02 AY28, Ireland
1359 Broadway, 12th Floor, New York, NY 10018, USA
E-mail: info@ospreypublishing.com
www.ospreypublishing.com

OSPREY is a trademark of Osprey Publishing Ltd

First published in Great Britain in 2026

A catalogue record for this book is available from the British Library.

ISBN: PB 9781472871046; eBook 9781472871053;ePDF 9781472871022; XML 9781472871039

26 27 28 29 30 10 9 8 7 6 5 4 3 2 1

Maps by bounford.com
Diagrams by Adam Tooby
Index by Richard Munro
Typeset by Lumina Datamatics Ltd
Printed and bound at Repro India Ltd.

MIX
Paper
FSC FSC® C047271

Osprey Publishing supports the Woodland Trust, the UK's leading woodland conservation charity.

CONTENTS

THE FLEET'S PURPOSE

In the early afternoon of 21 October 1805, the enigmatic Adm Horatio Nelson lay dying on the deck of the HMS *Victory*, mortally wounded by a musket shot from the French warship *Redoutable.* Nelson would not live to see the victory over his French and Spanish enemies. Of the combined Franco–Spanish fleet of 33 ships that joined battle off Cape Trafalgar, 17 struck their colours and the *Achille* exploded after sustaining crippling damage during the battle. Nelson's death occurred at the culmination of an Anglo–French war that raged across the Mediterranean for over 12 years. In 1793, the Mediterranean 'fleet' consisted of a small squadron designed to provide convoy security and protect British interests. By 1805, the Royal Navy possessed a dominant position in the Mediterranean, backed by the strength of maritime infrastructure and a financial commitment from Whitehall. This 12-year war saw a relentless commitment to gain control of the 'Middle Sea'

Along with battles, frigate warfare and the allure of treasure always captured the popular imagination of British society. The action of 16 October 1799, in which two Spanish treasure ships were captured by four British frigates, combined to make it one of the most impactful small actions of the war. Jervis' effective blockade of Atlantic-facing Spanish ports, including Cádiz, made the capture of these two valuable ships possible. (Bridgeman Images)

by the British naval apparatus. Trafalgar was only a point of inflection of this concerted effort by the British government to overcome its naval rivals and transform the nature of the French war.

The journey to dominance in the Mediterranean is not a story simply defined by naval battles. Battles in the Age of Sail were regularly fickle events, driven by uncontrollable conditions of weather and the willingness of both adversaries to risk an engagement. While the Nile and Trafalgar are significant events that dominate popular imagination, the more complete story of British dominance derives from a war of attrition. The ability of the British government and Royal Navy to apply pressure on the French and Spanish fleets over time ultimately led to the conditions of the late Napoleonic Empire: the Continental Blockade on British goods on the Continent, enforced by the French army. This attrition occurred in battles, but it also occurred through blockades, smaller ship actions, amphibious operations and economic warfare. The story of the British Mediterranean Fleet is one of a comprehensive strategy to suffocate the enemy, a process that took over a decade to achieve and not without significant defeats and disasters.

THE REALITIES OF WAR AGAINST FRANCE AND SPAIN

The requirements on the Mediterranean Fleet at a time of war were immense, as the diversity of the region generated significant demands. Shallow waters off the coast of Spain, France and the Italian states emphasized the primacy of littoral combat. Island chains and narrow straits in the Mediterranean created a premium on amphibious warfare and ship-to-shore bombardment. Control of critical chokepoints and shipping lanes offered as much opportunity for success without the risk of open battle. As in all eras, fleets constituted a massive expense on the British budget. Losing ships in combat and accidents increased domestic scrutiny and a burden on the public coffers. The dangerous weather and large inlets across the region provided sanctuary for fleets, giving the defender a significant advantage, often bringing coastal defences into play. Smaller warships were critical in interdicting trade and convoy escort, as larger ships of the line lacked manoeuvrability in pursuit. The fleet also required the ability to fight large engagements, as the Spanish and French – two traditional adversaries bound by the Bourbon Family Compact – remained a persistent threat throughout the period.

The Mediterranean war was also one of contingency. It is disingenuous to consider the French and Spanish fleets as punching bags or plot devices in a relentless march towards British naval hegemony. The Royal Navy almost lost the empire in the later stages of the American Revolution and was embarrassed repeatedly in that conflict. Commanders during the War

THE MEDITERRANEAN THEATRE

The French Revolutionary Wars became a truly global conflict because of naval power. Spanish and French naval power presented a threat to British commercial interests in the Mediterranean. French ambitions led to fighting over the 12-year period from the Acre to the Straits of Gibraltar for control of the region, alliances and markets.

of the First Coalition remained nervous about French naval power, despite historical postscripts about the Revolution destroying the French navy and the officer corps. France won victories at sea during the Revolution, and the French army often relegated British naval power to a sideshow up to 1798. Combined with Spanish naval power, the region was extremely dangerous for British captains between 1796 and 1799. British convoys were captured in the region, hurting economic power. This war for the Mediterranean was not simply a one-sided affair.

Other fleets played a role in the outcomes in the Mediterranean. The Neapolitan fleet augmented the British fleet during the siege of Toulon and remained relevant through the Second Coalition, if only to protect the vital straits around Sicily. The Spanish fleet during the First Coalition conducted independent actions against the French, participated at Toulon, and protected the Spanish coastline. The Portuguese fleet provided ships in support of the Maltese partisans in September 1798, until Nelson could bring more forces to sustain the siege of Valletta. The Russian and Ottoman fleets during the Second Coalition laid siege to Corfu for four months in 1798–1799, capturing the city. Russian naval power provided support to Neapolitan and British armies in Italy. Outside of 1796–1797, as the First Coalition collapsed, the British Mediterranean Fleet never operated unilaterally in the region and the theatre was never wholly defined as an Anglo-French conflict.

Additionally, the region was awash with maritime trade from countries all over Europe. Early in the Revolution, neutral powers played a critical role in transferring French trade across the region. Italian and French states relied on imported grain from other states. The Barbary States, perfidious entities in the region, provided grain and other commodities to European states while also engaging in piracy and hostage-taking activities. The swirling complexities of international trade-blurred lines of international norms made naval warfare complex for British captains. As a trend, British attacks on neutral shipping, formalized in the Orders in Council in 1793, systematically smothered third-party carrying trade. Napoleon's efforts to close off European ports offered a counterweight to these oppressive maritime policies, squeezing neutrality out of Europe between 1793 and the Peace of Tilsit in 1807.

Another critical aspect of understanding the value of the Mediterranean Fleet is its relation to other theatres of war. Between 1793 and 1805, the Mediterranean Fleet enabled activities in other theatres. Successful Mediterranean operations

HOLY ROMAN EMPIRE
FRANCE
SWITZERLAND
AUSTRIA
ITALIAN PRINCIP. (AUS)
KINGDOM OF SARDINIA
VENICE
GENOA
Genoa 1795
Marseilles
Hyères 1795
PAPAL STATES
Toulon 1793
Corsica 1794
CORSICA (FR)
OTTOMAN EMPIRE
KINGDOM OF NAPLES
PORTUGAL
SPAIN
Port Mahon 1798
KINGDOM OF SARDINIA
Mediterranean Sea
KINGDOM OF SICILY
Cape St Vincent 1797
Assault on Cádiz 1797
Cartagena
Trafalgar 1805
Gibraltar
Algeciras 1801
MALTA
Malta 1798 – 1800
BARBARY STATES
NORTH ATLANTIC OCEAN
MOROCCO
Acre 1799
Aboukir 1801
Nile 1798
OTTOMAN EMPIRE
Santa Cruz 1797
N
0
300 miles
0
300km
10° W
0°
10° E
20° E
30° E
50° N
40° N
30° N

protected the Channel Fleet and provided security to the Home Islands, particularly after 1799. Suppression of enemy naval power in Mediterranean ports provided opportunities for operations in the West Indies. The Mediterranean provided a layer of defence, particularly between 1798 and 1805 when the French government entertained a cross-Channel attack. Fleet operations were also concentrated around Gibraltar and the Portuguese coast when Franco–Spanish naval power gained control of the Western Mediterranean. At times, the Admiralty rebalanced warships between the three theatres based on emerging threats and enemy fleet mobilizations. It terms of resources and priorities, the Mediterranean Fleet never operated independently of activities in the West Indies, Channel and North Sea.

GREAT BRITAIN IN THE EARLY MODERN MEDITERRANEAN

The growth of British influence in the Mediterranean matched the expansion of trade in the region in the 17th and 18th centuries. With access to markets in Italy, particularly Leghorn (modern Livorno), and trade expansion in the Eastern Mediterranean, particularly at Smyrna (modern Izmir), the Levant Company experienced significant growth of its trade routes in the region. While, initially, the Levant Company provided its own trade protection from Barbary pirates and privateers in the region, the Royal Navy increasingly assumed the role of guarantor of trade in the 18th century. These methods of trade and maritime security led to roughly ten per cent of all British trade passing through the Mediterranean during the period. Particularly in times of war, the navy provided warships to conduct convoy escorts and apply military pressure to the political entities in the region. When war broke out in 1793, British merchants petitioned the government, making trade protection a critical consideration for the Admiralty.

Geopolitics also mattered. Since the 17th century, successive British governments held a principle of controlling the great seaways of Southern Europe. Following the Peace of Utrecht (1713), Great Britain gained an arbiter's position in the region, with the application of military power to maintain order. Two overarching geopolitical problems eroded this position of dominance. First, the Bourbon Family Compact, originally signed in 1733 and renewed during the 18th century, aligned French and Spanish strategic objectives, making efforts to promote British interests in the Mediterranean difficult. Second, British overseas colonial interests demanded the expansion of transatlantic naval power, minimizing the resources committed to the Mediterranean. The French Revolutionary Wars were not a confirmation of British strategic imperatives, but an attempt to return to a previously held position of strength guaranteed by Utrecht 80 years earlier.

By its geography, the Mediterranean offered opportunities. The Western basin, between Gibraltar and Sicily, held the predominance of enemy naval power. Chokepoints at both locations allowed naval squadrons to disrupt trade and arrest military movement. As the preponderance of Spanish and French naval power resided in Mediterranean ports, Carthagena and Toulon offered opportunities for blockade. The Royal Navy could hold strong positions at any of these locations and deny access to colonial markets. Iberia and the approaches to the Mediterranean also played a critical role in fleet activities. These approaches offered a location to threaten French and Spanish colonial trade. For a state dependent on gold and silver from Central and South America, naval victories in the Western Atlantic impacted the Spanish economy and war effort. Winning the war in the Western Mediterranean allowed the victor to exploit markets and military endeavours in the Black Sea, Syria, Turkey and Egypt. A variety of naval powers considered a canal through Suez, dating back to the Venetians in the 16th century. The Eastern Mediterranean offered ambitious opportunities for the state that could retain control of the seaways to the Levant. The relative weakness of naval powers in the Eastern Mediterranean also offered opportunities for alliances without risk of escalation.

The Ottoman protectorates on the Northern coast of Africa, often called the Barbary States, were a useful tool of British foreign policy. They executed their own trade of grain and goods from North Africa. The Barbary corsairs suppressed the carrying trade of smaller countries, which France and Spain used to bypass British blockade restrictions in times of war. British policy sought to court and maintain the independence of the Barbary States as a proxy. They even supported Barbary wars, as when the Bey of Algiers laid siege to the Spanish city of Oran in 1790. The Barbary States posed little threat to British

Gibraltar marked the gateway that linked the Mediterranean theatre with the transatlantic theatre. Due to the proximity of Càdiz and Cartagena, much of the fighting between the Spanish and British fleets took place around Gibraltar. While 'the Rock' received significant improvements during the war, Nelson's victory at Trafalgar reduced the need to invest more heavily in the port. The Admiralty would revitalize facilities at Gibraltar in the steam era with the opening of the Suez Canal. (Guildhall Library & Art Gallery / Heritage Images / Getty Images)

warships, but they preyed on merchant shipping and seized Christian slaves. The fledgling United States almost went to war with three different Muslim states on the African coast between 1794 and 1799. It finally fought a four-year war against Tripoli in 1801. The periphery of the Mediterranean provided cumulative resources for the European naval power willing to invest the energy in leveraging proxies.

By these dynamics, the Royal Navy was a revisionist power in 1793. The natural state of the Mediterranean was one dominated by Spanish and French naval power and, to a lesser extent, Ottoman and Russian fleets. The region was one of trade, and states in North Africa and the Ottoman Empire naturally aligned with economic interests to provide stability. As with Europe in general, the expansionist policies of the French Republic and the introduction of the Royal Navy in the region combined to overturn the existing order.

TO DEFEND AGAINST OR ATTACK THE FRENCH REPUBLIC?

The reasons that led British politicians and admirals to commit to the Mediterranean during the French Revolution are diverse. Initial British assessments before war broke out in 1793 deemed that the constitutional monarchy in Paris would generate a more favourable economic and political environment in Western Europe. Concerns about the dangers of the French Revolution, as voiced publicly by Edmund Burke (the politician and forefather of conservatism), were rare. As Prussia and Austria went to war with France, the radicalization of French politics led to the death of Louis XVI and the declaration of the French Republic. The newly established National Convention declared '*la Patrie en Danger*' (the Fatherland in danger) and deployed armies to fight along France's frontiers, make territorial gains and to liberate foreign populations from their monarchies. Efforts by the ministry of William Pitt the Younger to stay out of the war failed in late 1792 when the French Republic declared the Scheldt Estuary in the Austrian Netherlands open to commerce, a clear threat to British interests. French invasions into Savoy and Nice brought appeals from powers in Italy for the Royal Navy to defend Sardinian and Austrian interests.

At the outset of the war in the spring of 1793, the purpose of the fleet remained defensive. Encouraged by solicitation from wealthy merchants, the Admiralty committed naval power to increased trade protection in the region. The emergence of Spain as an ally in March 1793 offered an opportunity to break the Bourbon Family Compact for the first time in 60 years. French naval power, stationed at Toulon, offered an inviting target for blockade. What the Pitt Cabinet was unwilling to do was commit to regime change or invasion of French territory. *Émigré* appeals to support the young Louis XVI went unanswered. Pasquale Paoli, the Corsican nationalist, courted the British government for the navy to intervene in Corsica. His requests were ignored. The Mediterranean Fleet cruised off the French coastline in the summer of 1793 as a military force, as a defensive measure to protect order and British interests.

Adm Samuel Hood's decisions in the summer of 1793 transitioned the fleet's purpose from defensive to offensive. He made appeals to the Federalist revolt in Marseilles and Toulon; a group committed to constitutional monarchy in the middle of the Terror. To support the Federalists, he made declarations in support of Louis XVI, promoting his own political commentary to foreign courts in the region. As a part of counter-revolutionary efforts, he seized the French fleet and the harbour of Toulon in August 1793 to provide safehaven for the Federalists and a base of operations into France. In February 1794, he laid siege to San Fiorenzo on Corsica in support of Paoli, launching a four-month campaign across the island to eject the French garrison. Both operations were in French territory, as Corsica was annexed by France in 1769. Hood turned the Mediterranean Fleet from a defensive force into one committed to regime change. These policy objectives, eventually endorsed by the Pitt Ministry, defined the British goals in the region through 1795: seize French territory and encourage a counter-revolution in France.

Samuel Hood. A famous officer for his victories at the end of the American Revolution, Samuel Hood served as the first commander of the Mediterranean Fleet during the First Coalition. His declaration of support for the Federalists at Toulon, a counter-revolutionary statement the Pitt Ministry hoped to avoid, proved controversial. He destroyed only a portion of the French fleet at Toulon in December 1793. He captured Corsica in 1794, winning a series of amphibious victories. However, he failed to arrest the expansion of French armies at the expense of Spain and Sardinia and showed little interest in the diplomacy of the region, preferring unilateral efforts. The government forced him to strike his flag in 1795 as he fought openly with the Admiralty over reinforcements to the Mediterranean. (Kean Collection / Getty Images)

However, military defeats in the Alps and Pyrenees led to redefining the purpose of the Mediterranean Fleet. French expansion in 1796–1797 undermined allied efforts to contain Republican armies inside their borders. After Spain withdrew from the war in 1795, and Napoleon's victories in Italy in 1796, the Mediterranean Sea became much more dangerous. Adm John Jervis, the Earl of St Vincent, sought to maintain the tentative foothold in Gibraltar, contest French and Spanish power when possible, and blockade enemy fleets when possible. Napoleon's invasion of Egypt and the Levant provided an opportunity to reassert British maritime power as France overreached in the region. The War of the Second Coalition proved a period of British resurgence in the Mediterranean.

AN ANGLO–FRENCH WAR

By 1798, the War of the First Coalition transformed into an Anglo-French war. The combined power of France and Spain put British maritime power at risk. The aspirations of Napoleon and Lazare Carnot to invade Egypt and the Middle East posed a threat to British India and future designs on trade routes. Napoleon even held fanciful designs to partition the Ottoman Empire, giving

France a significant stake in the Eastern Mediterranean. Reintroduction of the fleet back into the Mediterranean offered an immediate counter to French ambitions and a bolster to potential European partners, including Austria and the Ottoman Empire.

The course of the war on land and sea proved the 'Whale versus Elephant' dynamic. France increasingly dominated European territory, extending its expansion into Germany and Italy during the War of the Second Coalition. At sea, Great Britain settled into a strategy of attrition based on two means: the Royal Navy and the power of financial subsidies to support the Second Coalition of Austria, Russia and the Ottomans. Pitt understood the value of long-term debt that permitted the expansion of the Royal Navy and provided loans to allies. The logical strategy to fight the war was through a system of blockades. However, as French expansion continued, the blockading requirements increased, driving a continuous growth in naval power. The strategy sought to suppress French and Spanish naval power in their home ports, intercept colonial trade and seize colonies where possible. This process also sought to rapidly degrade the fighting qualities of the enemy fleets and deprive them of a source of merchant sailors. In contrast, Napoleon sought to focus on colonial and maritime affairs when he gained the levers of power in France. The new French ruler increasingly recognized the requirement for his army to fight an economic war against Great Britain. Expansion of the French Empire would grow the coffers in Paris and deny European markets to British merchants.

The shortcomings of British strategy are clear. First, the British government chose to fight a protracted war. This required a significant commitment of naval power to the Mediterranean. It also forced dependence on the continental allies to do their share of fighting against French armies, reliant on British subsidies. This created tension with the Austrian and Russian courts about the lacklustre commitment from Great Britain, a problem remedied late in the Napoleonic Wars with Wellington's army in Iberia. Second, it required a firm commitment from the political base to commit national treasure to the war. Weathering the allied defeats on the battlefield and increasing political resistance, Pitt and his cabinet guided this strategy for over a decade. Even the short administration of Henry Addington (1801–1803) recognized the need for continuous preparation and commitment of naval forces, even as the combatants danced around the uneasy peace treaty signed at Amiens in February 1802.

Throughout the conflict, protection of the home island remained a vital national interest. Napoleon repeatedly sought to invade England from 1798 to 1805, a condition that required the growth of home forces. Addington, often chided as a peacemaker, raised over 370,000 volunteers in England and Ireland by 1803 to offset a threat of invasion. The construction of Martello Towers on the Channel coast, a fortification learned from the Mediterranean Fleet's operations in Corsica, provided locations to rally defenders against a landing. The aggressive cruising of the Channel Fleet and blockading of Brest and Boulogne made concentration of Napoleon's naval power to transport his army difficult. For the second half of the French Revolution, the Mediterranean Fleet and the Channel Fleet became more connected due to the risk of French and Spanish fleets combining to force a cross-Channel invasion.

Great Britain and France resumed the war in 1803 and fought continuously until 1814. Blockading of Toulon and the Spanish military port of Cádiz remained a central task for the Mediterranean Fleet. Spain was forced back into the war in December 1804 after a squadron of British frigates seized over one million pounds of gold and silver from treasure ships off Cádiz. At the outbreak of the War of the Third Coalition, the Mediterranean Fleet sought to maintain control of the combined forces of Spain and France, prevent their rendezvous with Napoleon's Army of Boulogne on the English Channel, and continue to attrit enemy naval power. These dynamics led to the Trafalgar campaign, the culmination of a decline in French and Spanish maritime power since 1793.

Unfortunately for British leadership, success at sea was matched by French successes on land. Victories of the *Grande Armée* at Ulm in Bavaria (16–19 October 1805) and Austerlitz (2 December 1805), combined with André Masséna's invasion of Naples, effectively crippled the Third Coalition. Worst, Napoleon gained access to Italian ports, with Austria ceding Venetia to the French satellite Kingdom of Italy. British interests now turned to protecting the Ottoman Empire, maintaining access to Vienna, and applying pressure to French ports and trade across the region. The war of blockade and economic strangulation would spread across Europe, from Portugal to Russia, as the character of the war changed.

FLEET FIGHTING POWER

William Hotham. Hood's second in command in the Mediterranean Fleet for the first 18 months of the war. Hotham assumed command in November 1794 when Hood returned to England for the winter and commanded throughout the 1795 campaign season. He fought the French Toulon fleet at indecisive actions off Genoa in March and Hyères Bay in July. Hotham made a commitment to fighting as a part of a combined force with the Austrians and Sardinians, but the disorganization of the allies and the deteriorating situation across the Mediterranean prevented Hotham from committing the fleet to the Ligurian coastline. (Wikimedia Commons / The Founding Collection / Public domain)

To emphasize the aggressiveness of British naval officers, it was a long-held belief that the French and Spanish possessed superior ship design technology during the period. British historians, influenced by the Enlightenment, held the scientific and philosophical attitudes of French society in high regard. Superior enemy ship design offered a way to excuse defeat and laud victory as a triumph of will over technology. Furthermore, early historians often considered this a period of a naval arms race with opposing fleets being built for the same purpose, akin to the Anglo-German naval race before World War I. The reality of warship design is more complicated and reflects shared designs and commonality as opposed to superior technology or better leadership.

In reality, Spain and France held different shipbuilding priorities. By the mid-18th century, both states recognized the unlikely opportunity of wrestling control of the oceans from the Royal Navy. Better opportunities existed in protecting lines of communication, colonial trade and achieving local superiority. Following the War of the Spanish Succession, where the Spanish navy was almost destroyed, 40 years of naval construction focused on defence of the empire and countering amphibious operations. Recognizing the weaknesses of the state and its position as a junior partner to France, Spanish naval administrators focused on a fleet that could escort trade and impose unacceptable costs on their enemy. In France, warships actually trended towards smaller ships of the line. With more resources but similar mandates, administrators committed significant investment in smaller, more manoeuvrable 74-gun third-rate warships, instead of massive three-deckers. Mid-century, the French naval administration focused on designing ships for speed, sacrificing bulk, as the theory went, increasing manoeuvrability and carrying firepower higher in the water. There is evidence to suggest that these efforts failed to produce the desired effect, while putting them at risk to British broadsides. French ministers and admirals recognized the risky nature of naval battle and the lessons of past wars in attempting to fight toe-to-toe with a British fleet. In situations fitting French design, such as the Mediterranean, their ships could exploit their manoeuvrability. However, French-built ships struggled in difficult weather conditions and in the line of battle.

The British Admiralty held different geopolitical priorities. Ship construction in the Royal Navy in the 17th century focused on large first-rate ships of the line to battle the Dutch. As the empire expanded, requirements changed. To range from the New World to India and dominate European waters, warships required versatility and endurance. Unlike the French and Spanish, British admirals desired durable, all-weather ships capable of cruising long ranges. Blockade duty required large holds to maintain provisions for extended periods. The efforts of Sir Thomas Slade, the Admiralty's ship designer in the 1760s and 1770s, created a fleet to meet these requirements. Under a new political administration

The Tragic Career of the HMS *Courageux*

The career of the HMS *Courageux* is an example of the long history of service of wooden sailing ships when properly maintained. Originally a French warship, the 74-gun third rate was commissioned in 1753 by the Bourbon government in a flurry of admiralty commissions in the aftermath of the War of the Austrian Succession. Captured in a fight off Cape Finisterre that same year, it was badly damaged in the fight with the *Bellona*, losing over 200 French sailors in the battle. It was commissioned into the Royal Navy in 1764, after almost two years of repairs were required to make the ship battle worthy. She underwent periodic repairs in 1773 and 1779. For a period of time before the American Revolution, *Courageux* served as a guardship at the mouth of Portsmouth harbour.

At the outbreak of the American Revolution, *Courageux* played a critical role in the capture of prizes in the Channel. In April 1781, she joined the force to relieve Gibraltar during the Spanish siege. At the end of the American Revolution, four 74s were ordered as copies of the *Courageux* based on the size and success of the French-built ship. In 1782 and 1787, the ship underwent further repairs, a testament to the long-term investment in warships. The ship was mobilized as part of the 1790 armament in response to the Nootka Sound Crisis (a clash between Great Britain and Spain concerning trading and navigational rights with the Spanish).

During the course of the French Revolution, the *Courageux* was one of the mainstays of the Mediterranean Fleet. The ship covered the landings of Hood's forces during the occupation of Toulon in August 1793. The ship was dispatched with Robert Linzee's squadron to attempt to force the French to surrender on Corsica. When French forces began storming Toulon in December 1793, the *Courageux* was undergoing repairs in the harbour. Without a rudder, the crew was forced to warp the ship out of the harbour to escape. In the battle of Genoa, the *Courageux*, along with the *Illustrious*, was in the van of Hotham's fleet in pursuit of Martin's French fleet. For much of the indecisive battle, the two British ships battled three French warships, *Duquesne*, *Tonnant* and *Victoire* for control of the disabled *Ça Ira*. The *Courageux* was heavily damaged in the fighting, losing two masts in the hour-long battle over the crippled French warship. On 14 July, similar circumstances brought the opposing fleets together off Hyères but they did not get into action.

The 43-year naval service of the *Courageux* ended in December 1796 in disaster. Anchored in Gibraltar following Jervis' escape from the Mediterranean, a violent storm broke the anchor line on the ship, causing her to drift wildly. Driven by the wind, she almost drifted under the Spanish guns outside the harbour, then drifted south toward the Barbary coastline. That night, in the middle of continued high winds, the *Courageux* was wrecked on the rocks below the Jebel Musa on the southern side of Gibraltar. In the disaster, 463 British sailors were lost.

committed to spending money on the navy, Slade and others dramatically changed the trajectory of the Royal Navy. It is arguable that the British did a better job in creating a fleet that matched their strategic requirements than the French or Spanish.

None of these naval advancements was done in isolation. During peacetime, French shipwrights travelled to British dockyards to examine new techniques. Exchange of ideas and technology continued as ships were captured on both sides. After the capture of French 74s at the Battles of Cape Finisterre in 1761, the British government turned to a line of battle more closely modelled on the French approach, with smaller warships. No power possessed a dominant position in technology at the outbreak of the Revolution. Naval technology was shared, stolen and universally applied in the 18th century. Shipbuilding espionage was rampant across the Continent. By the time of the French Revolution, most of the money and berth space at British dockyards was devoted to repairs of existing ships as opposed to building new ones. While the Admiralty expressed scepticism about Spanish and French designs, every enemy prize was commissioned because additional warships were needed. It also provided valuable propoganda for a French-named ship to fly British colours.

In the 18th century, the predominant battle tactic was the line of battle. As depicted at the battle of the Nile, British commanders desired an opportunity to bring their ships into close range of the enemy and mass firepower. British crews were better trained at gunnery than their Spanish and French counterparts. Close combat was stressed throughout the Royal Navy. (©Historical Picture Archive / Corbis / Getty Images)

SHIPS OF THE LINE

The ships of the line were the prestige ships, representative of British military power. In general, ships of the line were at least two-deckers. These warships could execute many of the tasks of smaller ships, such as escort duty, but their stated purpose was to stand in the line of battle and destroy enemy ships of the line. They were expensive investments for early modern states, particularly the massive 120- and 130-gun warships. The larger ships of the line could serve as floating headquarters for a port admiral or as a venue for diplomacy in a foreign port. Hood hosted the Federalist representatives on *Victory* outside of Toulon harbour as he negotiated the terms of the city's surrender. In combat, they never set the pace as they were slow and often difficult to sail, but they provided tremendous firepower and backbone; ships that could anchor a battle plan. Second-rate ships consisted of three decks and between 90 and 100 guns. The second rates as a class were in decline across the Royal Navy at the outbreak of the French Revolution, because they sailed poorly and lacked the size to serve as a flagship or floating embassy – something prized in the first-rate ships. The type survived the Revolutionary and Napoleonic Wars but never played a significant role.

Line of battle was the premier tactical formation in European navies since the mid-16th century. By the Revolution, the third-rate ships-of-line became the preferred battle platform in the late 1770s. 74-gun ships were the smallest ship expected to stand in the line of battle, capable of holding its own against ships with 40 or 50 more guns. There were exceptions, including the *Leander* (50 guns) at the battle of the Nile and the *Agamemnon*, *Polyphemus* and Spanish *San Leandro* (all 64s) at Trafalgar. In contrast with the bulkier warship, the third-rate ships emerged as the most numerous and popular. As the Royal Navy moved to a smaller ship of the line modelled along the French tactical formation, it focused its construction on new classes of third rates. Thomas Slade's construction efforts focused on modifying successive third-rate designs,

The Arrogant Class

The 12 ships of the Arrogant class were designed by Sir Thomas Slade along similar construction dimensions as the previous Bellona class. The lower gun deck supported 28 32-pdr cannons. The upper deck was designed to carry 28 18-pdrs. The *Arrogant* and *Cornwall* were ordered in 1758, but no additional ships were built on this design until 1774. The majority of the 12 ships were built during the American Revolution. The Mediterranean career of the class was extensive. Ships from the class fought at Cape St Vincent and the Nile. The *Bellerophon*, launched in 1786, took Napoleon's surrender when he came aboard after Waterloo in 1815. Only two ships of the class were lost due to combat: the *Cornwall* was burned in 1780, after successive battles in the West Indies during the American Revolution damaged her beyond repair. The *Illustrious* was damaged during the battle of Genoa in 1795. Under tow following the battle, one of her cannons blew a hole in the hull after an accidental discharge. Attempting to anchor near Leghorn, she ran aground and was burned.

building consecutively the Bellona, Arrogant, Ramillies, Albion, Elizabeth and Culloden classes in the decades between the Seven Years War and the French Revolution. Ships from these Slade designs played a major role in the Mediterranean war, forming the backbone of the fleet. Captured warships also played a critical role. For example, the French 80-gun *Tonnant* was captured twice – at Toulon and the Nile – and stood in the line of battle at Trafalgar against the Franco-Spanish fleet.

FRIGATES

Frigates, commonly considered fourth or fifth rate, served the most glamorous role in the fleet and proved to be the most useful ship design. While larger ships of the line remained with the fleet, the frigates operated independently. Their primary use was to execute patrols, commerce raiding and escorting convoys. As the frigate also served as the primary tool for fleet reconnaissance and security, the expectation in the Royal Navy was that frigate captains brought enemy frigates to battle. The frigate was large enough to carry significant armament but designed for speed and manoeuvrability. It could regularly avoid battle with larger warships. British frigates were designed to be all-weather, with their guns positioned on the upper decks. This allowed frigate captains to be aggressive because armament remained above the swells in rough seas. The size of the frigate led to the design being championed by privateers as well. Some of the frigates captured by the British during the course of the wars were 'irregular' forces as the French government turned to commerce raiding. Winning the frigate war offered an opportunity to seize convoys, dominate reconnaissance and provide assured security to the squadrons of larger warships. French-built frigates made up three-fifths of the British frigate fleet by 1801, with over 206 enemy frigates captured over the course of the French Revolution. The Royal Navy often sought to turn these ships against the enemy, despite concerns about inferior construction and lagging repairs.

Sir Sidney Smith. One of the more colourful and controversial figures of the era, Sir Sidney Smith led a wild life. On his own volition, Smith served in the Swedish navy and fought at the battle of Svensksund in the Baltic Sea in 1790. He led parties to burn the ships and stores in the evacuation of Toulon. He was captured at Le Havre and imprisoned in Paris in 1796. He assisted in repulsing Napoleon at Acre and supported the landing of Abercromby's force at Aboukir in 1801. (Chronicle / Alamy)

SMALLER CRAFT

Bomb vessels and gunboats

The Mediterranean Fleet also employed specialized ships for supporting bombardments and the destruction of ships at anchor. The Royal Navy was by its nature not a littoral navy and early in the war did not prioritize these capabilities. The transatlantic requirements of the naval service and the rivalry with France and Spain led to a navy built around the rated ships. This led to consequences when forced to conduct bombardments for amphibious operations or control of shallow waters. Hood and Nelson both expressed frustration in 1794 with the lack of shallow-draft ships to be able to cut littoral commerce and bombard modern fortifications. In Liguria in 1795, Nelson's squadron watched as the French Army of Italy shuttled troops and supplies up the Genoese coastline without being able to interdict these smaller vessels in shallow water. At the battle of Loano in November 1795, French shallow-draft vessels bombarded Austrian battalions from the sea outside of the reach of British warships.

When the Revolutionary Wars broke out, the Royal Navy only possessed two bomb ketches: the *Vesuvius* and *Terror*. Both ships were already over 25 years old. The Admiralty built no new bomb vessels until 1804, when the Convulsion class of bomb ketches were constructed. The bomb vessels that served in the Mediterranean during the war were purchased and captured, then converted to provide a unique capability. The HMS *Strombolo*, originally a mercantile vessel, was present at the surrender of Malta in 1800. In March 1801, the *Tartarus* and *Fury*, also converted merchant ships, supported the landing of Abercromby's army at Aboukir. Gunboats were smaller vessels, usually denoted by a cannon mounted forward or aft. The crew had to steer the gunboat into position to fire. They were extremely useful for close-in work against fortifications or ships at anchor. The first six purpose-built gunboats of the 1805 class were dispatched to Gibraltar for harbour protection.

Fireships

A time-honoured tactic in naval warfare, the term 'fireship' could apply to any ship used as an incendiary to attack enemy ships at anchor, sowing chaos and damaging the enemy for relatively little cost. The Royal Navy designed and built fireships in the 17th century, but the tactic died out until the American Revolution. Admirals Richard Howe and Richard Kempenfelt lobbied the Admiralty to bring them back, but demanded that the main requirement for the fireships was that they could maintain pace with the fleet. Nine ships of the Tisiphone class of fireships, designed in the 1780s, were built to support the fleet. When Sidney Smith evacuated forces from Toulon in 1793, the *Vulcan* was deployed with shore parties to ignite the French fleet and the arsenal. *Tisiphone* and *Conflagration* sailed with the Mediterranean Fleet but were never used in combat. *Incendiary* was captured in 1801 by Ganteaume's fleet near

Cádiz. Fireships became more popular with the Channel Fleet as the threat of Napoleon's invasion from Boulogne lingered in 1803–1805.

Schooners and cutters

The Mediterranean Fleet maintained its complement of smaller vessels, armed with carronades or a small armament of cannons. These ships regularly served as dispatch carriers but could also execute patrols and provide limited reconnaissance. It is also important to consider the privateering and irregular naval forces that prowled the periphery of the Mediterranean. These irregular forces often operated smaller vessels, but wealthier owners sailed frigates. While not regularly acting in conjunction with the Mediterranean Fleet, these forces contributed in small measure to the war effort. Privateering and capturing prizes remained a powerful aspect of maritime character for all combatant nations, but naval warfare had become more professional over the course of the 18th century. Privateers still patrolled coastal waters, some manning rather large warships. Most of these privateers manned small vessels, but some of the most infamous manned small frigates, a significant threat to isolated and unprotected shipping. As regular forces remained blockaded, France turned increasingly to commerce raiding as an attempt to offset British power. Unfortunately, privateering was akin to winning the lottery. Taking prizes proved difficult and the attrition rate among privateers was very high, fighting in waters against escorts, professional ships and shore batteries.

Troop transports

British practices in previous conflicts were the use of contracted transports from the merchant marine, a way of economizing costs in peace and wartime. In a time-constrained operation, gathering these merchant vessels could be costly and unresponsive. In contrast, the French often converted their own warships for troop transport. Beginning in the 1790s, the British government began the process of converting smaller warships, no longer capable of fighting in the battle line, into troop transports. These ships could still fight off a frigate or smaller vessel with a complement of guns, but the interior was designed to maximize stores and troops with a smaller crew to man the ship.

TECHNICAL FACTORS

Accidents

Over 90 per cent of all losses in the Royal Navy during the period resulted from accidents. For rough numbers of casualties, disease and individual accidents accounted for the death of upwards of 80,000 British sailors in the Napoleonic Wars. Roughly 13,000 British sailors died in shipwrecks and onboard fires between 1793 and 1815. Enemy action accounted for around 6,500 deaths. Shipwrecks proved the greatest killer of seamen, with at least 84 wrecks between

A print after TM Waller (1797), one of the officers of the ship, this illustration depicts an explosion of HMS *Boyne* on 1 May 1795 (V/ Adm Sir John Jervis' flagship, in action in the West Indies in 1794). This ship burned to the water's edge, and grounded on the Horse Shoal near Southsea Castle in 1795. Fortunately for the crew of the *Boyne*, when the smoke from the ship was identified, other ships off Spithead sent boats to save the crew. As a result, only 11 sailors died in the accident. In the print, the *Royal William* and *La Sybille* are also depicted as part of the rescue effort. (Incamerastock / Alamy)

1793 and 1815. The Mediterranean was well-known as a difficult region to sail due to the frequency of storms. Much of the Mediterranean was uncharted, leading to accidents when ships ran aground on unknown reefs and shoals. For example, as Nelson's captain built the battle plan for the Nile, they realized they had a problem. Between all of the ships in the fleet, they possessed a decades-old map of Aboukir Bay, a wildly incorrect British atlas and a sketch provided by a merchant captain. They ultimately relied on taking soundings and allowed local pilots to navigate the force into the attack. Jervis' evacuation from Corsica in 1796 was marred by the loss of the *Courageux* in a gale while anchored at Gibraltar, losing the majority of the crew on the rocky coast of North Africa. The command had four other ships damaged in the same storm.

Fires also remained a major fear for captains. Ten warships were lost during the Revolutionary and Napoleonic Wars to fires, but the impact on the Mediterranean Fleet was significant. The third-rate *Ardent* was mysteriously lost off Corsica in 1794 while on patrol. Only a portion of ship was ever found. Evidence suggested an explosion sank the ship and killed the entire crew. Jervis' 98-gun flagship, *Boyne*, was lost to a fire and explosion at Spithead on 1 May 1795. While most of his crew was saved, it delayed his arrival in the Mediterranean. The greatest naval accident in the Revolutionary Wars occurred with the loss of *Queen Charlotte*. The 110-gun warship was serving as Lord Keith's flagship for the Mediterranean Fleet. On 17 March 1800, it caught fire off Leghorn. American ships anchored nearby vainly attempted to come to the aid of the British ship, losing a number of sailors as the guns of the *Queen Charlotte* sympathetically fired in the intense heat. Keith, ashore in Leghorn, could only watch as the ship exploded, killing 673 officers and men. In 1796, one of Nelson's ships in the squadron off Liguria, the *Peterel*, caught fire. Fortunately, the sloop's crew rapidly responded by putting the fire out before it reached the magazine. Fire and explosions constantly concerned captains in the period; a hazard of wooden ships and magazines full of explosives.

In contrast, the French fleet lost 377 ships to enemy action over the course of French Revolutionary and Napoleonic wars and only 24 to accidents. The difference in experiences is stark when appreciating the effectiveness of the British blockade. The Mediterranean Fleet was forced to occupy risky positions outside the roads or in the harbour. In an era without clear navigational charts or global positioning, occupying these stationary or cruising positions placed many ships in harm's way. The price of the effective strategy and the attritional pressure on the enemy fleets put expensive ships and crews at significant risk. Much of the lack of accidents in the French and Spanish fleets can be attributed to sailing in home waters and captains being unwilling to leave harbours for risk of encountering British warships.

Sailors and marines

Foreign sailors made up a significant portion of the Mediterranean Fleet. On the *Victory* at Trafalgar, eight per cent of the crew were foreigners, comprising 12 different nationalities. During the war, the Mediterranean Fleet ran its own recruiting drives and press gangs at Italian ports and Malta, recruiting for their individual ships. While the complement of sailors proved satisfactory, the contingent of marines was lacking. The Mediterranean Fleet was undermanned; particularly during the first years of the Revolution, Hood and Hotham relied on army companies afloat on warships to fill those roles.

Mutiny was a constant concern for commanders, driven by long periods at sea. Pay for sailors in the Mediterranean Fleet was wildly infrequent and regularly contentious. Problems with delivering pay on a regular basis and the low pay to sailors became one of the fiercest complaints in the Revolutionary period, leading to mutinies across the fleet. The *Audacious*, a 74-gun warship, sailed to the Mediterranean in 1797. Its sailors were paid for the first time in 1801. The most famous mutinies of the period occurred at Spithead and the Nore in the spring of 1797. However, the Mediterranean Fleet suffered under the risk of mutiny, particularly during blockade duty where lulls in the action created idle sailors. In 1793, one of the ships in the fleet, the 74-gun *Berwick*, mutinied over the quality of rations. On 10 November 1794, the crew of *Windsor Castle* mutinied over the appointment of Capt William Shield as their

commander. Adm William Hotham, the commander of the fleet, considered using his marines and soldiers to storm the ship but decided to avoid bloodshed through negotiations. As a result, Shield and two junior officers were replaced to satisfy the demands of the crew. Jervis worried about mutiny outside of Cádiz and Cartagena during blockade duty, leading to aggressive action to keep sailors occupied. Jervis, a strict disciplinarian, hanged the ringleaders of a mutiny on the *St George* on 9 July 1797 outside of Cádiz, two days after the incident. It led to a shocking Sunday morning spectacle where one division of the fleet was fighting Spanish gunboats, one division was engaged in prayers, and the third division executed two mutineers. Jervis' tough hand on mutineers in the 1797 mutinies across the Royal Navy led to a number of ships being sent to the Mediterranean to steady their captains and crew under the watchful eye of the tough commander. However, disgruntled crews continued. Even some of the smaller ships and boats struggled to keep their crews satisfied. The crew of the *Albanaise* bomb vessel mutinied and sailed the brig into Malaga in 1800 to surrender it to the Spanish.

The fleet's crews excelled at naval gunnery. British commanders committed a great deal of energy training crews on the delivery of broadsides, which gave them an advantage in battle and in smaller engagements over French and Spanish crews. British crews were trained to deliver a high volume of fire,

The destruction of the *Queen Charlotte* in 1800 was one of the major accidents of the war. In the explosion, Keith's flagship lost 673 sailors despite efforts from American crews to save her crew. In this painting, the HMS *Speedy* is conducting salvage operations following the disaster. (The Picture Art Collection / Alamy) and speed of drills was the primary objective of commanders. Accuracy was extremely difficult to achieve at sea. Nelson's dictum that 'no captain can do very wrong if he places his ship alongside that of the enemy' was important because a captain willing to close the distance between his ship and the enemy ship could negate the impact of rolling seas on accuracy. Increased distance between ship and target induced waves and the roll of the ships into the equation. With some notable exceptions, British commanders were expected to close the distance with the enemy and risk casualties to inflict maximum damage from their broadsides. There were no established gun orders in the Royal Navy, as there was a manual of arms in European armies, but there was a common list of commands to direct the actions of crews. Most crews trained by dry-firing cannons, but notable exceptions included *Victory* at the start of the Revolutionary Wars, who regularly trained on live ammunition. This commitment to training, and an emphasis on fortitude in the face of enemy cannon fire, made most British warships lethal at close range.

With an emphasis on inflicting maximum damage and shock on an enemy ship, boarding in battle was rare and often required ships to collide while the enemy still had a means to resist. Engagements at close range often proved enough to force an enemy to surrender. Close ranges often brought muskets and pistol fire between decks into the fight. Despite the rarity, crews were organized to execute boarding of an enemy vessel. Boarding was a young man's game, usually led by a lieutenant instead of the ship's captain, but Nelson led his boarding party in the battle of Cape St Vincent, and other captains were willing to risk their lives to lead sailors and marines onto the deck of an enemy ship.

HOW THE FLEET OPERATED

COMMAND AND CONTROL

Behind the Home Fleet, the Mediterranean Fleet became the premier command over the course of the Revolutionary and Napoleonic Wars. In 1795, the fleet had 31 ships, including five first- and second-rate ships of the line. Two years later, the command swelled to 62 ships, the largest command in the Royal Navy. The fleet commanded by Jervis possessed 23 ships of the line and 24 frigates. The fleet continued to grow throughout the Napoleonic era. By 1810, the command possessed over 90 warships, a tremendous force to manage blockade and trade duties across the breadth of the Mediterranean.

Personalities played a significant role in how the fleet was commanded. Favouritism and personality defined the Mediterranean Fleet. The dynamics of command were complicated, even in a service known for a strict manner of command and directives. Paternalism and parochialism led to family trees in the officer corps, where senior officers nurtured and protected their favourites. Hood, known for being irascible, regularly played favourites with his captains and commodores. He fought openly with the army throughout his time in command. Nelson was a favourite of Hood. Hotham and Nelson disliked each other. Nelson loved Jervis. Nelson and Cochrane hated each other. The cliques that formed around these personalities defined internal dynamics and the relationship with the Admiralty and even Parliament.

The first group of leaders of the fleet possessed limited experience in the Mediterranean, reflective

PREVIOUS PAGE
Horatio Nelson. Nelson defines the Mediterranean Fleet's efforts between 1793 and 1805. He was seemingly everywhere during those 12 years, involved in most major fleet actions and amphibious operations. He also played a critical role in diplomacy with the Kingdom of Naples. The ubiquitous hero, Nelson helped create a generation of aggressive and ambitious naval officers. He also generated his share of feuds and controversies with fellow senior officers, commanders and government officials. Nelson's cohort of officers, particularly many of the junior captains, spent large portions of their career during the Revolutionary and Napoleonic Wars in the Mediterranean. As the Mediterranean Fleet grew over the course of the conflict, his influence on junior officers expanded. (Ann Ronan Pictures / Print Collector / Getty Images)

of the declining nature of European waters in the second half of the 18th century. There is a story – perhaps apocryphal – that when war broke out with France, the Admiralty searched for a naval captain who had sailed the Eastern Mediterranean and into the Dardanelles as so few of the senior naval officers had any experience in that region of the world. Hood's experience before the war was in the North Sea and Atlantic stations, winning his barony in the West Indies in the second half of the American Revolution. He also served in the Admiralty and as a member of Parliament, reflecting his high standing in Pitt's party. His experience in the Mediterranean at the outbreak of war was limited. Some of his subordinate admirals had served junior positions in the Mediterranean, but nothing like the experience gained by a generation of captains who would fight the war.

In contrast, Hotham's successor was John Jervis. The last time Jervis was in the Mediterranean was in 1772 as a young captain. However, Jervis travelled extensively in Northern Europe and Russia before the American Revolution. He also had experience in negotiations with the Genoese and aided in the three reliefs of Gibraltar (1780–1782) during the Spanish siege. At the outbreak of the French Revolutionary Wars, the Admiralty promoted Jervis to Vice-Admiral of the Blue and he was given command of the Leeward Islands. He transported Charles Grey's army to the West Indies in 1794. The expedition was controversial. British troops captured Martinique, Guadalupe and St Lucia, but ultimately lost Guadeloupe in a French counterattack. Many of Grey's troops ultimately succumbed to yellow fever and other tropical diseases in the expedition. Scandal ensued over the prize money tied to the French colonial possession, rankling members of Parliament. Jervis was promoted but failed to gain political clout and wealth due to such significant victories.

The Orde–Jervis Feud

When Napoleon sailed for Egypt, Jervis dispatched Nelson with a squadron to pursue the French, a chase that would culminate at the battle of the Nile. Against the backdrop of Nelson's hunt of Brueys in the Eastern Mediterranean, tempers flared with the fleet's leadership. When Jervis chose Nelson, R/Adm John Orde, who was senior to Nelson and third in command of the fleet, filed a complaint with Jervis over seniority and wrote bitterly about the lack of consideration and the favouritism of the commander. Jervis, enraged at a subordinate questioning his decision-making, ordered Orde to sail back to England. Orde refused, writing to the Admiralty Board requesting a court-martial to clear his name. The Admiralty Board refused the request. Orde then asked the Admiralty Board to court-martial Jervis for failing to support him. The Admiralty again refused the request. Infuriated, Orde challenged Jervis to a duel. The fight became so public that George III intervened, directing Jervis to decline the duel. The Admiralty solved the problem by censuring Jervis for his lack of consideration for Orde, but Jervis and Nelson were held in high regard at home following St Vincent, so no additional actions were taken against any of the officers. Because of the incident, Nelson hated Orde. The rear-admiral, for his part, never had any ill feelings toward Nelson. He admitted he only sought to maintain the traditions of sea service and the officer corps.

George Elphinstone, Lord Keith, served as Jervis' second in command in the Mediterranean from 1798 and assumed command of the fleet in November 1799. Keith had been with Hood at the capture of Toulon before serving outside of the Mediterranean. His major contributions included cooperation with the Austrians to capture Genoa in 1800, and the convoy and amphibious operation to Egypt in 1801. He commanded the fleet to the Peace of Amiens.

Lost in the Trafalgar narrative and the War of the Third Coalition is Adm Richard Bickerton. The admiral, who was seemingly everywhere but the Mediterranean during the first seven years of the war, arrived in the theatre escorting the 21,000-man army to Egypt. He commanded the *Swiftsure* on blockading duty outside Cádiz and blockaded Menou's army in Alexandria harbour in 1801. He oversaw the repatriation of French troops after the surrender. After Amiens, he assumed command from Keith for a period of time, then served as Nelson's second in command. He blockaded Toulon and assumed temporary command while Nelson pursued Villeneuve to the West Indies before Trafalgar.

Adm Cuthbert Collingwood, Nelson's successor, proved to be an excellent choice to maintain pressure on the French and Spanish fleets. He maintained the blockades of Cádiz, Cartagena and Toulon, forcing back into port numerous attempts to run the British blockade. Additionally, Collingwood excelled as a diplomat, making missions to Morocco, Naples and Constantinople. He dispatched forces to skirmish in the Dardanelles to keep the Ottomans out of the War of the Fourth Coalition, and eventually negotiated face-to-face with the Sultan in 1807. Collingwood excelled at the military and diplomatic requirements of his command until he succumbed to cancer in 1810, securing the gains he won alongside Nelson at Trafalgar through patience and consistency.

George Elphinstone, Lord Keith. Before assuming command of the Mediterranean Fleet, Keith captured a Dutch squadron near the Cape of Good Hope and helped suppress the Nore mutinies. His time in command was marked by the Second Coalition, support to the siege of Genoa and support to Abercromby's army in Egypt. (Universal History Archive / Getty Images)

Centralized control of naval forces proved almost impossible. Spanish and French governments held all the advantages in communication in the Western Mediterranean, with distances from ships to shore and communication lines to the capitals relatively short. In contrast, communication with direction from Whitehall took weeks, either from packet boat dispatch or through an overland route through Europe. As French armies expanded in Germany and Italy, communications routes became less reliable. The Mediterranean commander became dependent upon his experience and network of captains and diplomats to gather intelligence and provide directives.

It was equally difficult to command the fleet at sea. Even in the relatively tight confines of the Mediterranean, losing contact with a ship or an enemy squadron was common. Control of the fleet required intent and aggressiveness to overcome the friction of the decentralized nature of operations. Direction for patrols and movement of squadrons provided general guidelines. Signals from the admiral mattered, but initiative and intent also factored into decision-making. For the naval commander operating away from the fleet, interpretation and improvisation often determined a course of action.

The officer corps in the Royal Navy was semi-professional, by modern standards. Nelson's signal at Trafalgar that 'England expects every man to do his duty' was an ambitious statement because the character of the sea service remained somewhat ambiguous. While the Royal Navy was more professional than the era of Vernon and Anson a few decades earlier, naval warfare encouraged what modern military standards might consider amateurish or semi-piratical behaviour. The pursuit of prize money, a life-altering reward, was always a consideration for officers who, by law, stood to gain a significant share in the sale of a captured ship and cargo. However, modern elements of professionalism existed. In an era where naval battles proved difficult to initiate, let alone win, meteorological conditions or enemy decisions led to accusations of dishonour and disobedience. Often these public criticisms led to two outcomes: a public outcry in Parliament or a court-martial. Many commanders were willing to make personal appeals to the Admiralty to protect themselves from scrutiny. On rare occasions, commanders published pamphlets in London to justify their actions. Loss of a ship or failure in battle led to points of honour and public accountability. When the *Berwick* lost her lower mast over the side during a refit in San Fiorenzo Bay in 1795, the captain, first lieutenant and master were all relieved during a hasty court-martial.

Undergirding these dynamics of command was the unreliable intelligence collection apparatus and communications system. The Royal Navy depended

Deck action during a battle was chaotic and full of danger. A commander's willingness to close with French and Spanish ships put himself and the crew at great risk, reliant on training to overcome the dangers of the opposing ship. (©Fine Art Photographic Library / Corbis / Getty Images)

on collection from a variety of sources – diplomatic agents, spies, foreign courts, merchant shipping, allied commanders and their own ship captains – to collect information and interpret it into actionable intelligence. In the Mediterranean, it proved difficult to determine the enemy course of action, causing regular panics as the fleet commander dispatched ships across the region to regain contact with French and Spanish squadrons. In an era where human intelligence was the only form of collection, the speed at communicating intelligence to decision-makers could be lengthy. Overland, it could take weeks to send dispatches to Whitehall from the Mediterranean and receive a response. As the French Republic expanded, continental communications became strained. By packet boat through the Straits of Gibraltar, winds and weather could disrupt communications. Enemy ships could intercept these light or unarmed vessels. Even if the message made it to London, there was no guarantee that the communication could be interpreted and actioned promptly.

In contrast, the National Assembly committed to Claude Chappe's semaphore system across France in 1790 to support rapid military communications. By 1794, *Le système* Chappe could communicate from Paris to the frontiers in under ten minutes. Spokes of this system expanded to all fronts during the war, rapidly expanding the speed of decision-making. The system was valuable in the defence, but when French ambitions expanded beyond the boundaries of the Republic, French naval commanders suffered from similar lengthy communications problems, ambiguity and friction. Communications between theatres remained flimsy and lengthy, making coordination extremely difficult.

Warfare on the Continent shaped the Mediterranean due to a variety of factors. Because of the elongated timelines for sailing vessels and communications around Spain through the Straits of Gibraltar, naval warfare required the precise allocation and composition of forces. Decisions made in London were difficult to reverse. Continental theatres, particularly in the Alps and Pyrenees, influenced the length and focus of the naval campaigns. Extreme weather, in winter and summer, slowed campaigns to a crawl in both theatres. Campaign seasons had a rhythm in the Mediterranean, with the winter season leading to pauses in naval operations and a period of skirmishing and observation. Changes in the allocation of forces to the Mediterranean often came during these pauses; opportunities to reassess the military and diplomatic situation. As the war expanded beyond the Alps and Pyrenees, war became more ubiquitous.

The Mediterranean Fleet was structured as a traditional maritime force of the period. Tactically, the fleet was broken down into divisions – a van, a body and a rear – to allow the fleet to fight in multiple directions. Admirals commanded from their flagships, but command of the ship usually devolved to a captain to allow the admiral to focus on fighting his entire formation. A signalling system, championed by Howe and Kempenfelt, allowed admirals to signal commands to the other ships in their divisions. Frigates and smaller ships provided security for the fleet or detached squadrons, serving in a reconnaissance and security

On 21 April 1800, the Austrian army laid siege to Genoa, occupied by French Gen André Massena and 28,000 troops. Keith blockaded Genoa from the seaward side in support of the Austrians and used gunboats to bombard the city's defences. Massena held the city until 4 June, providing ample time for Napoleon to manoeuvre over the Alps into Lombardy. (DeAgostini / Getty Images)

capacity. Intelligence networks, managed through spies and diplomats, provided early warning of French and Spanish mobilization and the departure of warships.

It is incorrect to consider naval warfare of the period as a concentration of forces that moved around the Mediterranean seeking battle. Hunting and pursuing enemy ships created a very dynamic theatre. For commanders, naval warfare was a process of concentration and distribution. When intelligence indicated the movement of a body of French warships or a convoy, a commander would bring what forces were available together for the opportunity of an engagement. When battle seemed unlikely, commanders maintained their forces across stations in the Mediterranean, maintaining coverage on a myriad of tasks and missions. Concentration required discipline associated with naval battle: signals, formations and a strict adherence to command. Distribution required individual captains to take action based on general orders, intent and initiative. The problem of concentration and distribution induced risks and opportunities through the Revolutionary and Napoleonic period. Battle was difficult to obtain at sea. Much like land warfare in the early modern period, pitched battle required commitment from both sides. Unlike land warfare, weather, seas and wind play a more critical role in determining the likelihood of battle. Jervis stumbled into two victories. Hotham deliberately attempted to bring the Toulon fleet to battle twice in 1795 and failed. Nelson caught an enemy fleet at anchor. Chance and luck played a role in determining outcomes, particularly in battle.

ADMINISTRATION, BASES AND LOGISTICS

The Admiralty learned from the war. While bureaucracy is often lamented as slow and cumbersome, the failures of the first few years of the war encouraged change in how the Admiralty managed the fleet. Much of the success of the Mediterranean Fleet can be attributed to the Admiralty leadership, who endeavoured to make the bureaucracy work and provide continuous support over distance. Charles Middleton, Lord Barham, is perhaps the most important contributor to success at the Admiralty. Barham did not excel as a naval officer, but he proved adept at bureaucracy and advocating for the navy. With his close relationship with Pitt in the decade between the American and French Revolutions, he stressed the need for continued investment in the fleet and infrastructure. In a period of political economy, the government's order of the construction of 12 ships of the line and 65 repaired between 1783 and 1789 was a huge achievement. Barham's goal of maintaining 90 battleships and 90 frigates provided a needed deterrence and put the Royal Navy on a solid footing when war broke out in 1793. In and out of office throughout the French Revolution, Barham provided advice to Pitt and Henry Dundas on naval matters and strategy. He maintained active correspondence with commanders at all stations and his experience provided him with ship-level knowledge of the Royal Navy. Contemporaries and historians credited him as the mastermind behind the Trafalgar campaign. He played a critical role in the inter-theatre requirements of managing an empire-wide war.

The tyranny of distance proved the most difficult problem for Barham and the Admiralty to overcome. Unlike Toulon, Cádiz and Cartagena, the best basing and dockyards were in Great Britain. The Mediterranean Fleet remained at sea, perhaps even years for some ships, without breaks. Hotham sent concerns to the Admiralty in late 1794 that many of the ships in the fleet had not had a refit in 17 months. Any major or 'great' repairs, as the Admiralty described overhauls of warships, required facilities not available at any of the smaller British bases in the region. For minor repairs, crews often made expedient repairs to keep their ships in action. For major repairs, ships were rotated back to British dockyards. British sailors would not see dry docks established in the Mediterranean until the mid-19th century with the construction of facilities on Malta.

During the 18th century, the Admiralty organized how the dockyards supported the fleets in time of war. Maintenance and repair of ships was concentrated at the larger dockyards of Portsmouth, Plymouth and the Nore. Riverside docks were used for outfitting and shipbuilding. Deptford on the southside of the Thames River served numerous functions: building of smaller ships, outfitting warships, handling stores and victualling. (Wikimedia Commons / Public domain)

As with the waning value of the Mediterranean Fleet before the French Revolution, the impact of Gibraltar on British strategy was not realized until the war was nearly three years old. In the first years of the Revolution, reinforcements and resupply came from depots like Deptford and Portsmouth. The journey was regularly delayed by weather. Once they arrived in the Mediterranean, they were at risk from French and Spanish warships until they rendezvoused with the fleet. As Hotham learned in 1795, the meeting between reinforcements and the fleet could significantly disrupt operations. Before the outbreak of war, naval logistics at 'the Rock' were conducted in an episodic fashion. The shortcomings of naval activities were identified as far back as the Seven Years War, but economizing the Royal Navy made improvements infeasible. In 1793, the Royal Navy established a commissioner to oversee naval stores and dockyard activities. Jervis' arrival at Gibraltar in 1798 invigorated efforts to make Gibraltar an offensive base. Under his direction, the dockyards were improved to provide repairs to ships in Mediterranean service. These dockyards proved valuable in repairing the British squadron defeated during the first battle of Algeciras in 1801. Jervis also directed the building of victualling yards and water reservoirs. These improvements stabilized logistics for the Mediterranean Fleet and provided a base of operations for the Nile campaign, the expedition to Minorca and the siege of Malta. In 1804, the government made a proposal to establish a permanent naval force at Gibraltar to protect the cruising squadrons, forward positioning supplies, and provide the command with an expeditionary capability. Trafalgar and the defeat of the Spanish navy negated a need to make further expansions in Gibraltar's capabilities until the mid-19th century with the opening of the Suez Canal. However, the war proved the value of Gibraltar as a location to project power and shorten supply lines.

As with all military logistics, the resupply of British warships was a detail-driven process. For the fleet in the Mediterranean, ship captains were always concerned about the arrival of stores of all supplies. During their times in command, Jervis and Nelson made significant efforts to shorten their supply lines to Mediterranean ports instead of relying on the significant naval logistics infrastructure in Great Britain. (The Print Collector / Getty Images)

Many of the other bases in the region proved episodic. Because of their location, other potential basing options held political and military considerations for France and Spain. Peace negotiations often centred on Great Britain returning these possessions as part of the settlement. Corsica never provided a viable long-term solution for fleet basing due to the geopolitical situation. The harbour of Ajaccio was selected and used for a period of time following the island's capture in 1794. San Fiorenzo Bay was used for minor repairs. A hospital was established on the island, initially catering for the soldiers and sailors who contracted disease during the seizure of Corsica. Jervis attempted to move the fleet to Elba after the capture of Porto Ferrajo,

'Port Mahon, Minorca with British men of war at anchor', John Thomas Serres (c.1795). One of the most disputed territories in the Mediterranean, Minorca offered tremendous benefits for the naval power that could capture and retain it. Port Mahon offered a secure harbour and its proximity to Spanish ports made it ideal for patrols and blockading forces. It was captured by Duckworth's expedition in 1798. Great Britain surrendered four years later to Spain as conditions for the Peace of Amiens. (Yale Center for British Art / Paul Mellon Collection / B1976.7.68 / Public domain)

but the deteriorating situation in 1796 forced its evacuation. Following the evacuation of Corsica, Jervis based the fleet out of the mouth of the Tagus in Portugal. For a period of time, Lisbon served as the home station until the French invasion of Egypt brought the fleet back into the Mediterranean.

Port Mahon on Minorca exchanged hands several times throughout the 18th century. The Royal Navy captured the island in 1708 and retained the island in the Peace of Utrecht at the end of the War of the Spanish Succession. In 1756, the Louis Francois du Plessis, 3rd Duke de Richelieu, captured the island in a two-month siege. In 1763, the British exchanged the colony of Guadeloupe with the French in exchange for the return of Minorca to British control. In 1782, Minorca fell again after a five-month siege by a Franco-Spanish force under the command of Louis des Balbes de Crillon. At the Peace of Paris the next year, the British government surrendered Mahon back to the Spanish after over 75 years of almost continuous occupation.

Gaining the advantage after the Nile, Jervis decided to launch an expedition to Minorca under the command of R/Adm John Duckworth on 19 October 1798. Charles Stuart commanded the 800 troops that constituted the storming party, supported by a squadron of three ships of the line and three frigates. The lightning operation overcame the defences of Port Mahon systematically, taking batteries and gun emplacements over the course of a week. Henry Paget, the future Earl of Uxbridge and Wellington's cavalry commander on the Peninsula and Waterloo, led an independent attack to gain control of Fort Charles, allowing Duckworth to bring his squadron into the harbour. In nine days, Spanish resistance collapsed. Duckworth and Stuart captured 4,000 troops, four Spanish frigates, and earned the fleet a valuable chess piece in the Mediterranean. Following its recapture, the personnel evacuated from Corsica were relocated to establish the base on Minorca. Mahon was a quality harbour,

NEXT PAGE
'Battle between *Ligurienne* and HMS *Peterel*, 30 Ventôse an VIII (21 March 1800)', Antoine Roux. Regardless of ship size, fighting often came down to the willingness of a commander and favourable weather conditions. The *Peterel* was a 16-gun sloop completed in June 1794. It served with Nelson's squadron off Liguria and was able to capture six smaller French vessels supporting operations from Toulon to Mantua. The ship participated in the capture of Minorca with Duckworth, executed anti-smuggling operations and served as a vessel to transport dispatches from the fleet to the regular mail packets. Francis Austen, elder brother of the author Jane Austen, commanded the *Peterel* in the capture of over 40 prizes during the War of the Second Coalition. (Wikimedia Commons / Public domain)

easily defended, with the stores and careening space to maintain the fleet. Minorca provided a valuable location to apply pressure on the Spanish Mediterranean ports and fortifications. However, it was surrendered in 1801 as part of the Peace of Amiens.

Victualling for the fleet proved difficult. Many of the meat, grains and milk products could be preserved. Fresh vegetables were perishable without refrigeration. Victualling also required precise consumption rates and meticulous accounting onboard the ships to avoid over requisitioning or running out of food. For the Home Fleet and other expeditions launched from home waters, the Victualling Board expected individual ships to come to rendezvous points with storeships to resupply food and other items. Deliveries could be made from Deptford to the blockading fleet at Ushant. For the Mediterranean Fleet, distances and travel times made victualling from Deptford storehouses even more difficult. At the outbreak of the war, Hood's command relied on agent-victuallers operating in neutral or friendly ports in the region to help supplement supplies from England. As the French Republic expanded, occupying forces closed Italian and Spanish ports

British Martello Towers

The impact of the Mediterranean war was felt throughout the British Empire as the fleet interacted with unique military engineering in the region. The Genoese first designed and installed a tower at Mortella Point near San Fiorenzo on Corsica in the 16th century. The tower offered a practical defensive position from seaward attacks and offered a way to link multiple towers together for mutual defence and signals. Robert Linzee's squadron tried to unsuccessfully dislodge the French at San Fiorenzo in the autumn of 1793. The fleet returned in February 1794 to seize Corsica from the French defenders. Hood reported back to the British government about the stout nature of the free-standing towers. In the storming of the defences around San Fiorenzo, 33 French defenders held the tower for two days under fire from the *Fortitude* and *Juno*, often at ranges as close as 150yd with only two 18-pdr cannons. The *Fortitude* and *Juno* even exchanged hot shots with the tower. After the intense barrage, Hood reported back to London that the French defenders only lost two soldiers in the engagement, a testament to the strength of the tower design.

In response to the effectiveness of the tower, the British government embarked on using the design to protect from a French invasion. From 1804 to 1812, the government built 103 Martello (a misspelling by the British) Towers to cover the coastline. MajGen William Twiss, a military engineer with experience during the American Revolution and continental campaigns, oversaw the construction of the towers. Charles Stuart also directed the building of 12 towers on Minorca during the British occupation. During the Bourbon protectorate on Sicily, the British government encouraged the building of towers on the island. In the 19th century, the British government copied the military fortification in India, Canada and as far away as Australia.

to victualling. As a result, the Mediterranean Fleet hunted for food through victualling agents further afield. By 1804, agents were making arrangements for food deliveries from neutral ports in the Ottoman Empire and Russia.

Health was also a significant concern for the fleet. The Admiralty, particularly Jervis, was an early convert to the large-scale procurement of lemon juice for the fleet. This practice practically eliminated scurvy in home waters. For longer cruises and ships stationed away from home waters, scurvy remained a fear. During the course of the war, the Mediterranean Fleet relied on the Sicilian lemon fields to protect it from scurvy. Nelson established the contract for Sicilian growers to provide 30,000 gallons of lemon juice a year. New recruits were washed and clothed on separate ships before joining their permanent crew, as the Royal Navy learned this was a way of reducing typhus in the fleet. Smallpox vaccinations were available but not heavily enforced by the Admiralty. The real killer in the fleet was tropical disease. The squadrons sent to the West Indies are the best-known victims of tropical diseases during the Revolutionary Wars, but the landing forces on Corsica in 1794 were wrecked by disease with much of the army regiments, marines and sailors sick by the surrender of Calvi. Outside of the Corsica campaign, sickness was rare in the Mediterranean Fleet. When the new fleet doctor arrived on *Victory* in early 1805, the Mediterranean Fleet had been at sea for almost two years and there were minimal medical concerns. Dr Leonard Gillespie reported only a handful of ill sailors in the entire fleet. Treatment of battle wounds and injuries lagged behind disease prevention. The Royal Navy had yet to begin the practice of triage, only treating wounded men

THE CAPTURE OF CALVI, CORSICA (overleaf)

In late July 1794, French defenders held the last bastion on Corsica, the citadel on Calvi. Calvi was heavily defended from the seaward side by the interlocking fires of Mollinochesco and Mozello. LtGen Charles Stuart sought to avoid landing at the face of the French defenders and decided on a landing at Port-Agra, west of Calvi. While the landing was four miles from Calvi, it was on the far side of a steep mountain range that required sailors and soldiers to haul artillery over the mountains. Trails were improved but much of the transportation of naval guns occurred with human muscle. Nelson estimated that many of these guns were dragged tens of miles up circuitous routes. Stuart's laborious manoeuvre bypassed the French defences and placed British improvised batteries on higher ground above the enemy fortifications. Aided by Corsican partisans and guides, the manoeuvre caught the French defenders offguard, with Stuart's troops able to close within 750yd of Mozello before opening fire with two mortar and four-gun batteries. On 6 July, Mollinochesco fell. Twelve days later, troops of the 50th Regiment of Foot, Royal Fusiliers and the Royal Irish Regiment stormed a breach in the walls of Mozello. On 19 July, Stuart's batteries opened on the French defenders in the citadel and the town. Over the next two weeks, the British and French batteries exchanged fire until the French commander agreed to surrender the city on 10 August. British casualties in the fighting were light, but Stuart's force was effectively crippled by the end of the siege due to malaria ravaging Corsica that summer. Nelson was also wounded in the fighting, losing the use of his right eye. The operations on Corsica, culminating in the capture of Calvi, provided evidence of the expertise of British amphibious operations and the utility of naval power to strike at weakened points of an enemy's defence.

A Martello Tower in Corsica guards a harbour prior to the Revolutionary Wars. The Mediterranean Fleet was impressed by the stout defence of the French defenders outside of San Fiorenzo during a raid in 1793 and the invasion of the island in 1794. The fortification design was copied across the empire. (The Picture Art Collection / Alamy)

by the order of arrival to the surgeon. As such, men who could have been saved often bled to death waiting on a doctor occupied with treating minor wounds.

Blockade duty

Blockade duty played an important role in the Mediterranean Fleet. Often, these blockades focused on the military ports of the enemy. Cádiz on the Atlantic side of Gibraltar, Cartagena just inside the Mediterranean, and Toulon in Provence. At other times, circumstances offered an opportunity to corner an enemy fleet, as Hotham did with Martin's fleet along the French coastline in 1795. Blockade duty was a double-edged sword. As the force blockaded, the fleet and crew suffered as sailing maintained readiness of the warships. As the blockading force, periods at anchor could lead to boredom. For a crew regularly unpaid, far away from home, and at risk of not receiving regular rations, conditions of a blockade could lead to mutiny. Blockading duty had its share of risk from accidents and storms as most blockades were executed outside of the cover of the harbour. Shore batteries also posed a concern for crews if set adrift by winds or weather.

Commanding at the blockade of Cádiz, Jervis took active measures to prevent mutiny. He believed in constantly training and maintaining a highly regimented schedule, despite the monotony of daily duties. He made tremendous effort to ensure fresh foods arrived for the blockading force at regular intervals, with the officers remarking about the regular mutton, fowl, eggs and vegetables from Portugal and the Regency of Tangiers. He rotated divisions out of the close blockade, keeping at least seven warships outside the harbour while cruising the rest of the fleet or anchoring them at Gibraltar.

Attacks on the Spanish fleet in the harbour of Cádiz offered multiple benefits. It kept the sailors in the fleet sharp. Jervis executed a number of raids with small boats into the harbour, hoping to goad Córdoba into action. If successful, the enterprising sailors of the fleet might catch the Spanish fleet on fire at anchor. In July 1797, Jervis attempted to push a bomb vessel into the harbour to bombard the fleet. In one of the most dramatic incidents during the Cádiz blockade, Spanish and British boats clashed in between the fleets. For a commander worried about the morale and loyalty of his men, the sharp action offered a way of maintaining focus.

Blockading duty could become very routine and almost cordial. Communication between ship and shore occurred discreetly, with correspondence exchanged in the middle of the night to avoid the fleet seeing opposing sides of the game being too familiar. Officers confessed to getting their linens washed by the ladies of

Cádiz during the blockade. Routine views of a city and its inhabitants provided a calming environment for crews regularly committed to rigorous duties in difficult conditions.

Blockades placed a tremendous strain on the enemy squadrons confined to the port. For the blockading force, observation of an enemy port offered a mix of boredom and terror. Blockade duty exposed the ships to storms and enemy attacks. Many crews became bored and, in some cases, mutinous. Commanders focused on discipline and training were necessary to keep ships and crews fit during long periods of blockade duty. (The Picture Art Collection / Alamy)

Hunting treasure fleets

Colonial wealth remained the backbone of the financial and economic power of the Spanish Empire. Even by the late 18th century, the Spanish crown relied on these transatlantic processes to support military and economic efforts in Europe. The process began with the mining of mercury in the Almaden mines in Spain, a location of mercury deposits known for over 2,000 years. Merchants transported the mercury to Spanish ports to be escorted by warships to the New World. In the colonial mines, the process of amalgamation – the combining of mercury with gold and silver ore – produced pure specie. This purified gold and silver would be loaded to transports for the return voyage to Spain. By the time of the French Revolutionary Wars, this process of exchanging Spanish mercury for colonial specie had been in place for over 200 years. While the Spanish had diversified the extraction process from mercury mines in Peru, the transatlantic exchange remained important to stabilizing the Spanish economy.

Frigates thrived in the world of convoy warfare. Frigates had the speed and manoeuvrability to transport gold and silver without fear of getting cornered by British warships. Frigates could also conduct reconnaissance to identify the arrival of a convoy and signal to a nearby squadron to intercept. Frigates were also willing to risk battle against other frigates. The frigates were the most glamorous posting in the Royal Navy. Led by intrepid captains and crews inspired by prize money, frigates occupied the popular imagination on all sides of the naval war. This was not just popular fiction. Captains dating back to the era of Drake and Hawkins hoped for an opportunity to capture a vast fortune on a Spanish ship. In earlier wars of the 18th century, squadrons had made these dreams a reality. While larger ships of the line hunted and escorted convoys on occasion, minor frigate actions could have strategic consequences.

Early in the Revolutionary Wars, Spanish treasure fleets were safe due to the alliance with Great Britain. However, with the withdrawal of Spain from the First Coalition, the hunt for treasure ships began anew. One of the major risks of treasure convoys in wartime was that conditions at Spanish ports could change rapidly with British blockades. With delayed communication, a port open two months earlier when the treasure ships left Veracruz could arrive at their destination with British warships waiting. On 26 April 1797, the 74-gun *Irresistible* and the Frigate *Emerald* encountered two Spanish frigates on the southern end of Jervis' blockade of Cádiz. The two Spanish ships, laden with silver, were bound for Cádiz but unknowingly sailed into the middle of the British fleet in the middle of the night. Realizing the risk to the treasure, the Spanish captains offloaded the silver into fishing boats before sheltering in Conil Bay near Cape Trafalgar. The *Irresistible* and *Emerald* gave chase and attacked the ships at anchor. Both ships surrendered after an hour and a half of broadsides. The ingenuity of the Spanish commanders saved the specie from falling into the hands of the British, as the fishing vessel was able to slip into Cádiz undetected from the blockading ships.

Two years later, the Spanish were less fortunate. Two Spanish frigates laden with over two million Spanish silver dollars attempted to enter Vigo on 15 October 1799 but were discovered by the blockading force outside the harbour. The 38-gun HMS *Naiad* gave pursuit, joined overnight by three other British frigates. The British frigates split the *Thetis* and *Santa Brigida*. One of the British frigates, *Ethalion*, fought the *Thetis* alone while the other three frigates chased *Santa Brigida*. The *Thetis* surrendered after an hour-long battle with the *Ethalion*. The *Santa Brigida* attempted to escape by wrecking its British pursuers on the rocky outcroppings of Cape Finisterre, but was eventually cornered and forced to surrender. With the Spanish frigates in tow, the four British frigates sailed for Plymouth. When they arrived, the scale of their victory was finally realized. The value of the cargo in the Prize Courts amounted to £618,040 (or over £61 million in 2025 value). Frigate captains were paid £150 a year. For the payment of their prize money, each received £40,730. The victory was feted across England. The specie required 63 wagons for transport from Plymouth to the Bank of England.

Contingency and confusion influenced naval operations. On 10 August 1805, Capt Thomas Baker, commanding the *Phoenix*, fell in with the French frigate *La Didon* off Cape Finisterre. In an engagement lasting a few hours, the *Phoenix* and *La Didon* were heavily damaged until British gunners dismasted the French frigate. The fight between two frigates had unintended consequences. First, Capt Pierre Milius carried orders for a French squadron to combine with Villeneuve's combined Franco-Spanish force. These dispatches never reached Brest. Even worse for the French, with the *La Didon* in tow, the *Phoenix* was spotted by Villeneuve's fleet as it attempted to enter the Channel. Evidence suggest that the presence of both ships concerned Villeneuve about British preparations and caused him to lose heart in forcing a passage. (Wikimedia Commons / Public domain)

COMBAT AND ANALYSIS

THE CAMPAIGN AT SEA

Military history must acknowledge contingency and context. The naval war played a role in the first three coalitions against France, of which the Mediterranean theatre played a significant part in understanding outcomes and consequences. The conduct of armies, treaties and political decisions played a role in the Mediterranean theatre. To separate naval history from the wider context of the war would skew the value of naval warfare and the fleet. The French Revolutionary and Napoleonic Wars are often analyzed by the series of seven coalitions. While the analysis of the Mediterranean Fleet covers the first three coalitions, the Anglo-French war continued almost unabated between 1793 and 1805. Anglo-Spanish tensions overlapped throughout the period. As a result, the Mediterranean theatre remained in a state of war or crisis throughout the 12 years from Toulon to Trafalgar.

It is necessary to look at the Mediterranean theatre in three distinct phases. The first period is one of French triumph, unlocking the Eastern Mediterranean and forcing the British from the region. The second phase involves a resurgence in British naval power, leading from the battle of the Nile to the Peace of Amiens. The third phase is the events of 1803–1805, leading to the triumph at Trafalgar and the transformation of the naval war against Napoleon.

Toulon and counter-revolution

At the outbreak of the French Revolutionary War in 1793, Great Britain maintained only a squadron in the Mediterranean. Hood was appointed to command the Mediterranean Fleet in March after the outbreak of hostilities. In June, he led the reinforced squadron from Portsmouth through the straits of Gibraltar and on to the French coastline. Hood's fleet was dispatched to the Mediterranean with defensive considerations, the protection of commerce and disrupting French maritime and trade considerations. French efforts to spread Republican ideology in the Italian states reinforced the importance of a *Cordon Sanitaire*, a concept first championed by the Spanish court in the early years of the Revolution. More aggressive operations, including attacks along the French coast, were discounted or secondary to the defence of the growing alliance. However, Henry Dundas, the Home and Colonial Secretary, desired aggressive operations at some point against Toulon or other French interests. As the diplomatic corps aggressively cobbled together alliances with the Sardinian, Neapolitan and Spanish crowns, future considerations included close cooperation between the fleet and allied armies operating in the Alps and Pyrenees; but those operations were considered for the spring of 1794, at the earliest. One consideration largely rejected was the promotion of a civil war in France or embracing *émigré* ideology. The Pitt Ministry considered the war one of traditional balance of power and interstate warfare, not one of regime change.

French internal politics intervened on British strategy. During the summer of 1793, the Federalist movement in southern France erupted. Initially formed as part of the urban uprisings in Marseilles, Toulon and Lyon, this movement sought to revert the French government back to the Constitution of 1791. French Republican armies responded violently, suppressing revolts in Lyon, Avignon and Marseilles in July and August. Federalist sympathizers fled to Toulon, turning the French fleet moored in the road against the Parisian government. The situation proved fortuitous for the desperate Federalist leadership, who initiated communications with Hood and the fleet stationed outside of Toulon. During a series of negotiations, Hood accepted the surrender of Toulon and the French fleet on 29 August in the name of Louis XVII, a decision that merged *émigré* interests with British strategy. It was a decision Pitt and the diplomatic corps desperately desired to avoid, considering the public statements by the British government against favouring a form of French rule. Hood backed up his declarations with an occupation of the port and city, reorienting allied troops to the lodgement inside France.

The four-month siege of Toulon by French Republican forces caused considerable problems for Hood and the alliance. The British admiral stressed the need for reinforcing the port in September and October 1793, drawing troops and ships from the Spanish, Sardinian and Neapolitan allies. By late November, it was becoming increasingly clear to British leadership that holding Toulon would be impossible as the French army methodically tightened the siege. (DeAgostini / Getty Images)

At the height of occupation, Hood's forces numbered over 23,000 troops, from British and allied forces occupying the fortifications around the port. For the coalition, Toulon represented both a valuable naval stronghold and an opportunity to cripple French maritime power. The arrival of British, Spanish, Neapolitan and Piedmontese troops turned Toulon into the centrepiece of Mediterranean operations, but it also drew immediate attention from the French Revolutionary armies. A Sardinian counterattack in the Alps and Spanish operations in the Pyrenees became sideshows to the control of the French military port. Dundas diverted troops destined for the West Indies to the Mediterranean in an attempt to reinforce a perceived victory.

The French Republic moved quickly to retake Toulon, dispatching troops under the command of Gen Jacques François Dugommier and, crucially, placing a young artillery officer, Napoleon Bonaparte, in charge of directing the siege. Bonaparte's strategic placement of artillery eventually forced the coalition to concede the position. However, by late November, it became clear that the allies would be unable to hold the city. By December 1793, French batteries dominated the approaches to the harbour, making it untenable for the British and their allies to remain. During the withdrawal on 17–18 December, the British and their allies sought to deny Toulon's naval resources to the French by destroying the fleet anchored in the harbour. They succeeded in burning or scuttling a significant portion of the ships. Approximately half of the vessels were lost or sailed out of the harbour, including several ships of the line. However, the evacuation was incomplete and disorganized; the French managed to save several warships, preserving enough naval capacity to rebuild their Mediterranean presence. The fall of Toulon thus marked a costly but decisive victory for the Republic, one that demonstrated the vulnerability of the coalition alliance and elevated Napoleon's reputation as a rising military strategist.

British efforts at Toulon gained very little. Hood missed the opportunity to steal the entirety of the French fleet. While some French stores and shipping were destroyed, the Republican government and the Toulon fleet recovered quickly. The political statement made by the British admiral forced the Pitt Ministry to acknowledge the internal politics of France and the radical nature of the Terror. Hood's actions at Toulon accelerated the pace and expanded the scope of the war. Hood's declaration of support for Louis XVII spread to foreign courts across the region and intensified the nature of the conflict. This was no longer a traditional 18th-century conflict, but one for the future of France. His actions moved Great Britain in line with the more radical counter-revolutionary politics of Spain and Austria, something the Pitt Ministry desperately hoped to avoid in 1793. Hood's actions also invigorated the National Convention, under threat from French Royalist factions and allied invasion, to take drastic measures to suppress rebellion and counterattack on all fronts.

Corsica campaign

The Federalists were not the only political entity to seek advantage from the arrival of the Mediterranean Fleet. Pasquale Paoli, the Corsican politician and revolutionary, sought to throw off the chains of French rule on the island. France seized Corsica in 1768, the year before Napoleon's birth. Paoli desired to use allied presence in the region as a pretext for an armed uprising against French rule. Corsica had a long and complicated political history. While its proximity to the French coastline and military theatres provided an attractive venue for basing a fleet, there were other strategic and political considerations. Before French rule, the Republic of Genoa had controlled the island since the Middle Ages. The British government made repeated unsuccessful attempts to use the island as a bargaining chip in the 18th century. Other states held flimsy claims on the island, including the Papal States and Spain. Any campaign on the island would incite animosity in the region and complicate the peace-making process following the war. Furthermore, the island maintained a semi-feudal mentality, dominated by families and factionalism. Uniting the island into a single polity through military force proved difficult.

Influenced by Paoli's pleas, Hood decided to intervene, citing its proximity to French shipping and Toulon. In February 1794, Hood began executing operations to eject the small French garrisons from Corsica. The fleet executed an amphibious landing and seized the batteries guarding San Fiorenzo, forcing the French garrison to flee inland to Bastia in the northeast corner of Corsica. The next operation seized Bastia on the northeast corner of the island on 22 May. With the capture of Bastia, the Corsican population rose up in rebellion and declared an Anglo-Corsican Kingdom with George III as its head of state. Operations continued in June with a daring land-sea operation to seize Calvi, the last French garrison on the island. By August 1794, Corsica lay in British hands in a largely unilateral campaign.

While the amphibious operations ended successfully, showcasing the skill in British amphibious warfare, Corsica exposed significant operational and strategic problems. The Mediterranean Fleet lacked the marines and army regiments to garrison an island and provide an amphibious capability to support the Spanish and Sardinians. Army and navy leadership clashed throughout the invasion, with the generals concerned over the risk associated in the operation and the lack of support from the fleet. The tensions led to the retirement of two separate senior generals and animosity among army officers serving in the fleet and the naval commander. Carlos III of Spain and Manuel de Godoy, his chief minister, expressed disgust at the operation on Corsica as a distraction and an intrusion on Spanish interests. As the French government considered Corsica an integral part of their country, the invasion of the island only exacerbated the rhetoric of Toulon. Finally, the Pitt Ministry installed Gilbert Elliot, a Whig politician, to serve as viceroy of Corsica, exacerbating the relationship with Paoli and the Corsican elites. The two-year history of the Anglo-Corsican kingdom proved a tumultuous one, leading to open clashes among senior leaders and political infighting between the British-led faction and the Corsican independence movement.

Collapse of the allied frontiers

While Hood focused his efforts on Corsica, the war continued in the Alps and the Pyrenees. While the Spanish Army of the Eastern Pyrenees (also named the Army of Catalonia) gained initial successes in the mountainous border between Spain and France, the French army experienced a resurgence in 1794. Defeat of the Federalists freed thousands of troops to move to the frontiers. Commanded by Dugommier, the French Army of the Eastern Pyrenees counterattacked in November 1794, leading to the important victory at Black Mountain, and the retreat of the Spanish army south. Over the next six months, the French army won a series of victories in pitched battles and sieges, forcing the Spanish to withdraw to a line along the Fluvià River. Fearing a collapse of the army and the fragile political system, Carlos and Godoy sought a political settlement, initiating dialogue with the French government in Basel in the spring of 1795.

John Jervis, Earl of St Vincent. Jervis arrived in the Mediterranean Fleet in late 1795 and assumed command of an almost untenable situation as the Spanish became French allies. His victory at Cape St Vincent was wildly feted across Great Britain, despite only capturing four Spanish ships. His commitment to the blockade eroded the Spanish navy and created opportunities for the Royal Navy to re-establish itself in the Mediterranean. One of his lesser-known contributions to winning the Mediterranean theatre was the expansion of Gibraltar's victualling and dockyard capabilities to sustain the fleet. (Universal History Archive / Getty Images)

The Sardinian front held longer but suffered from increased pressure from Republican armies. In the background of Hood's operations on Corsica, inconclusive fighting in the Alpine passes dominated the summer of 1794. The Sardinians benefited from a short campaign season as snowfall closed the Alpine passes from October to May. Disease was rampant in the French Army of Italy in 1794–1795, crippling formations and forcing the army to rely on an extended system of magazines and coastal fortifications extending along the Ligurian coast back to Provence. Despite these problems, the French army threatened to invade Genoa and break through the Ligurian Alps onto the plains of Piedmont. British diplomats feared the encirclement of Turin and the collapse of the Sardinian war effort. In response, Hood provided no tangible support to the defence of the Alps, remaining focused on securing Corsica as a base of operations throughout much of 1794. By the winter of 1794, fears increased in the British diplomatic corps that Sardinia might initiate peace talks with the Spanish.

Renewed Anglo-allied cooperation

In November 1794, Hood returned to London, citing ill health and a desire to use his influence to expand the commitment in the Mediterranean. While Hood secured Corsica in 1794, the British government launched the Grey-Jervis expedition in the West Indies to seize French colonies. The Pitt Ministry was making a significant strategy shift in committing troops and warships to seize French colonial possessions, an acknowledgement of a protracted war against France. Hood left the command of the fleet to Adm William Hotham, his deputy, during the first two years of the war, with considerable experience in amphibious operations. Nelson strongly disliked Hotham, who he considered timid, but the temporary commander proved attuned to the dangerous situation in the Alps and Pyrenees.

The fleet Hotham inherited was in disarray. Hood left the theatre on bad terms with the allies and in conflict with the diplomats on the course of the war. Many of the ships had been in rough seas for over a year and engaged in constant patrolling or blockade duty. Morale in the fleet was low. Hood was a secretive commander and shared little information with his subordinates. Hotham even lamented to the Admiralty that Hood took all his correspondence with him when he sailed to London, leaving Hotham without a paper trail to navigate the diplomatic and military situation. Herculean French efforts made the remnants of the Toulon fleet a viable force, compounding Hotham's concerns.

In response, the new fleet commander turned back to the allies. The threat of French invasion in Italy brought renewed interest from the Austrians in a counterattack to protect hereditary lands in Lombardy. In February 1795, the Austrian government hosted a conference in Milan to develop an operational plan for the Ligurian campaign season. The combined Austro-Sardinian army would sweep over the passes, encircling the French Army of Italy along the Ligurian coastline. Ambitious, the operation planned to destroy the enemy army with a rapid encirclement, pinning the French between allied armies and the sea. As a part of this operation, Hotham planned a blockade along the Ligurian coast, intercepting littoral vessels resupplying the French army from the sea and bombarding French fortifications. Hotham intended to hold the French army in place as the allied army could complete its destruction. If the allies could link an operation in Liguria with the emerging Royalist movement in the Vendee and Eastern France, a select group of British politicians and diplomats believed Republican France might collapse.

The plan ran into problems almost immediately. The French fleet, under the command of Pierre Martin, put to sea to conduct their own amphibious operations. Hotham turned his attention to the maritime threat, leading to an indecisive battle of Genoa in March. While Hotham's pursuit blockaded the French fleet near Antibes, he could not bring Martin to battle. British reinforcements sailed into the Mediterranean, forcing Hotham to divert the fleet away to ensure the French could not intercept the divided naval forces. Hotham also lacked the right fleet composition to support the allies. The situation required littoral ships and gunboats. Hotham lacked these vessels, making the interception of littoral trade and coastal bombardment on the shallow waters in Liguria difficult. The unravelling diplomatic situation only exacerbated the military struggles. Negotiations at Basel threatened to neutralize the Spanish fleet at best. At worst, it might bring the Spanish into the war on the side of the French. Over the course of the spring, the diplomatic situation forced Hotham to keep an eye on the Spanish naval forces in the Mediterranean. The Barbary States pivoted back to their traditional economic relationship with France, reopening trade lines to the chagrin of the captains committed to patrolling North African waters.

In June, the allies attacked Liguria. The allied attack was late and slow to materialize. The terrain did not support the ambitious plan, as the mountain passes were a struggle for artillery and supply wagons required to provide the army with momentum. Infighting between the Austrian and Sardinian commanders exacerbated tensions over a peace deal and long-standing concerns over unity in the coalition. Hotham arrived back on the Ligurian coastline as Martin made another attempt to intervene with the French fleet. Another running battle occurred around the Hyères Islands in July that proved inconclusive.

French Mediterranean Cruises of 1795

The situation in the autumn of 1795 became desperate for the Mediterranean Fleet and the Anglo-Corsican Kingdom. France and Spain signed the Peace of Basel in June 1795, making Spain neutral in the war, and freeing thousands of French troops for service in the Alps and Italy. The loss of Spanish naval support stretched the Royal Navy in requirements to maintain control of French ports. The Austro-Sardinian counterattack in Italy ground to a halt during the summer. Expectations were arising of a potential French counterattack before the Alpine passes closed for the winter. With an impetus on blockading Toulon, Hotham found his fleet being pulled in numerous directions to maintain control of trade and monitor Spanish developments.

The French naval situation also necessitated a change in plans. Martin's cruises in the spring and summer of 1795 put his fleet twice at risk of an engagement with Hotham. Losses in the Toulon and Brest fleets required a rebalancing of forces. The deteriorating situation offered an opportunity to menace trade across the Mediterranean and capture the British Smyrna Convoy. Martin received orders to direct a squadron to raid British commerce in the West Indies and the Atlantic. On 14 September, a squadron of six ships of the line and three frigates under the command of Joseph de Richery slipped out of Toulon and sailed for Gibraltar to escape the Mediterranean. A second squadron, under the command of Honoré Ganteaume, evaded the British squadrons in late September and sailed for the Eastern Mediterranean. Ganteaume was originally appointed as the squadron to seize the Smyrna Convoy, but his squadron missed the convoy, who already sailed past Malta in early October. Unable to support a close blockade of Toulon, Hotham found out about both expeditions well after Richery and Ganteaume escaped.

In the fortunes that coloured maritime warfare during the period, Richery stumbled into the Smyrna Convoy off the southern tip of Portugal. On the morning of 7 October, the Smyrna Convoy, escorted by three British ships of the line, encountered Richery off Cape St Vincent. Recognizing the size of Richery's force, the British commander signalled for the convoy to scatter and formed a line of battle with his three warships. Richery dispatched his frigates to chase down the convoy and joined the battle with his warships. In the three-hour battle, the *Censeur*, a French ship captured previously in the war, was crippled and forced to surrender. Richery called off the pursuit and collected 30 out of the 31 merchant ships in the convoy. The French fleet then sailed to Cádiz with the prizes and protection from the Spanish fortifications. R/Adm Robert Mann, dispatched with a squadron by Hotham to find Richery, blockaded Cádiz after finding the French fleet and prizes in the harbour.

Ganteaume's cruise was less dramatic but equally damaging to the British war effort. In October and November, his force cruised the Eastern Mediterranean, ambushing British and Neapolitan shipping around Smyrna. In the winter, Ganteaume's squadron was hit by a storm and almost trapped in the Dardanelles by a pursuing force under Thomas Troubridge. Escaping the British, Ganteaume returned to Toulon in February 1796 prior to the start of Napoleon's first Italian campaign.

The two French cruises in 1795 highlight the tenuous nature of allied naval power in the Mediterranean. The Spanish fleet had the power to help tip the scales in either direction. Their loss and the declining situation on the European continent overextended Hotham's fleet and risked commercial disasters.

Martin's efforts kept Hotham occupied, allowing French battalions to withdraw southwest down the Ligurian coast to prevent their capture. By late July, the operation ground to a halt with the French Army of Italy consolidated. In the autumn, the French conducted a counterattack. This time, Martin was able to provide his own gunboats to the operation, allowing the French army to win a stunning victory at Loano. The 1795 campaign season ended with the French army poised to attack into Lombardy and Piedmont.

Throughout the summer and autumn, Spanish intentions worried British leadership. Spain withdrew into neutrality on 22 July. Hotham and the diplomats believed it was a matter of time before Spain joined France, their traditional ally, to oppose British naval power in the Mediterranean. The fleet now needed to watch Cartagena and Cádiz for indications of Spanish mobilization. The war was becoming increasingly more dangerous as French armies swept their enemies from the First Coalition.

Defeat and withdrawal: 1796

The following year, the situation in Italy completely unravelled. Napoleon assumed command of the Army of Italy in March and immediately went on the attack. His victories at Dego and Montenotte broke the back of Sardinian resistance, unlocked the northern Alpine passes, and drove the Austrians back into Lombardy. As Napoleon attacked north into Italy, the British fleet assumed the role of bystanders in a war of manoeuvre, incapable of influencing the operations or logistical support of the French army. Nelson commented on his inability to stop French shipping in Liguria and the incessant flow of troops and supplies onto the Lombard plain.

John Jervis, the new commander, had no choice but to turn his attention to the emergence of a Franco-Spanish naval threat as Napoleon drove a wedge between Anglo-Austrian coordination. Gilbert, struggling to maintain control of Corsica in the wake of an independence movement and the collapse of the war effort in Italy, recognized the need to end the Anglo-Corsican

BATTLE OF CAPE ST VINCENT

Nelson's victory, arguably in the spirit of Jervis' order, won this battle, but there were other tremendous victories that day. Collingwood, in command of the *Excellent*, captured two Spanish warships. Troubridge on the *Culloden* raced ahead to save the *Captain* from being overwhelmed in the chaotic fighting in the middle of the day.

At the opening of the battle, the Mediterranean Fleet caught the Spanish fleet unprepared, with their forces split. Jervis formed two lines with the intent of passing through the middle of the Spanish fleet and destroying it in detail. The Spanish lee division made multiple attempts to break the British line to rejoin the division but were unable due to the speed of the fleet.

Jervis turned the fleet toward the Spanish windward division, directing the fleet to form one line. Nelson, breaking ranks, wore his ship out of line and began a pursuit on his own. As the *Captain* sailed into the middle of the Spanish division, it became engaged by six warships.

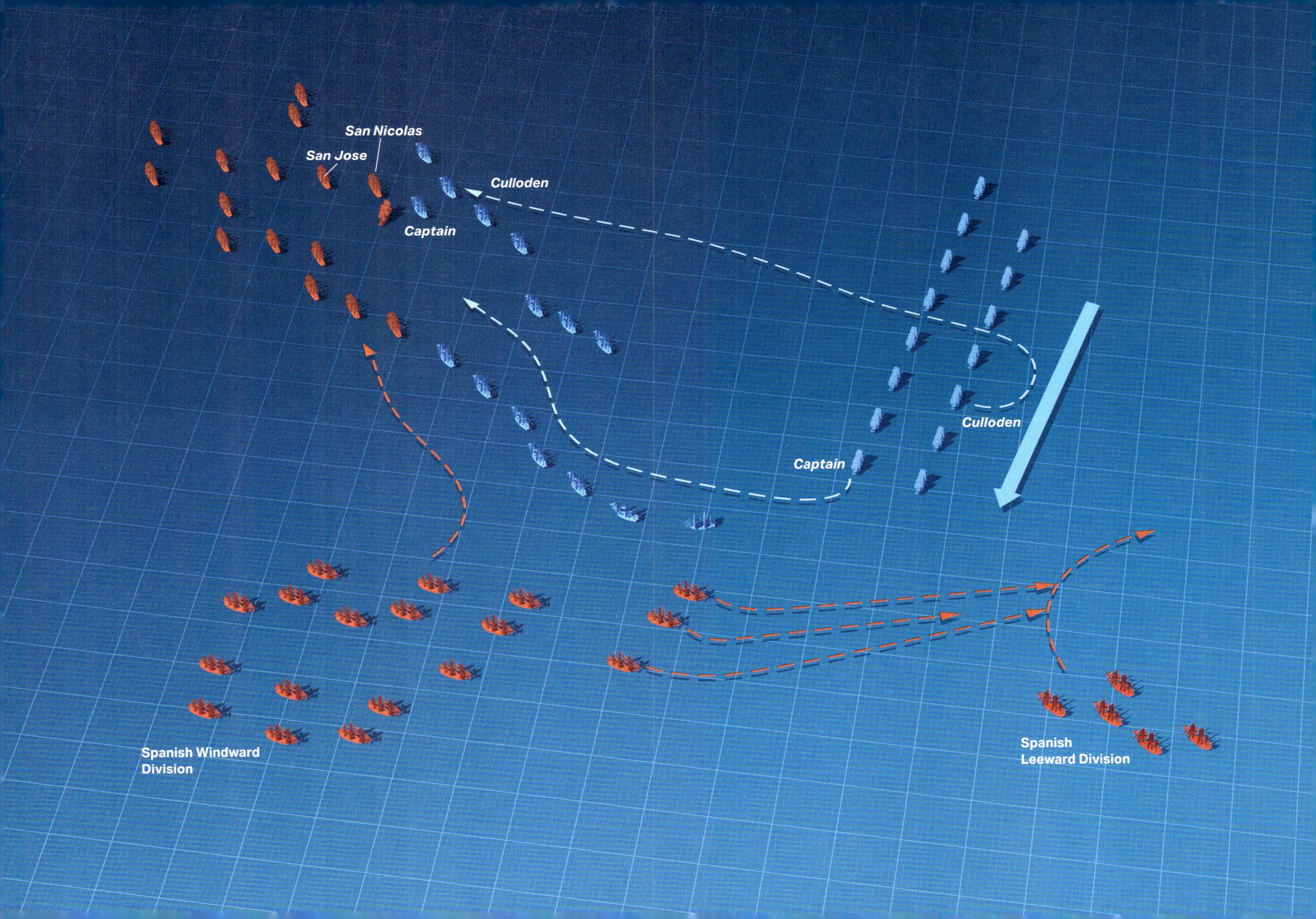

Spanish Windward Division
San Nicolas
San Jose
Captain
Culloden
Captain
Culloden
Spanish Leeward Division

government and evacuate the island. The French captured Leghorn on 30 June 1796. Nelson landed on Elba to reestablish a foothold and security buffer as French forces marched south on the Italian mainland. As French armies rampaged across northern Italy and toppled Austrian principalities, Spain declared war on Great Britain on 19 August 1796. Sensing the increasing risk of staying on Corsica and Elba, Jervis withdrew all forces from the Western Mediterranean, sailing for Gibraltar in November 1796. British forces on Elba evacuated in December, leaving no British warships east of Gibraltar by the beginning of 1797. The Mediterranean Fleet was now at the low tide of the war, having lost the Sardinian, Austrian and Spanish allies to the success of French armies. Jervis would fight on alone, stationing the majority of the fleet near Lisbon to wait for an opportunity to strike back at the Spanish and French.

Cape St Vincent

With initiative passing to the Franco-Spanish alliance, their strategy turned to protect their dominant position in the region. Spanish plans in 1797 included the combining of forces with the French to present a united front in the Mediterranean and ensure the protection of their convoys to their American colonies. Adm José de Córdoba moved his fleet from Cartagena on 1 February through the straits heading for the safety of Cádiz, but a strong wind blew them further into the Atlantic, preventing them from reaching the Spanish military harbour. While stuck off the coast of Cape St Vincent in contrary winds, Córdoba possessed a significant force with 25 ships of the line and seven frigates.

The stark difficulties of naval warfare played out over the next two weeks. Jervis responded aggressively to reports of Córdoba leaving Cartagena, but his tasks included collecting accurate intelligence on enemy movements, rendezvousing with reinforcements and bringing an enemy fleet to battle before it reached Cádiz. Jervis left the Tagus with only ten ships of the line. If he stumbled into a fight with Córdoba, he was woefully outnumbered. Fortunately, Adm William Parker arrived from the Channel Fleet on 6 February with five additional ships of the line. Parker was also fortunate to find Jervis instead of Córdoba. After the rendezvous with Parker's force, Jervis made every attempt to find the Spanish before they escaped the opportunity for battle. Nelson, sailing aboard the frigate *Minerva*, passed through Córdoba's fleet on 11 February, still struggling to get back to Cádiz, but he had no idea of the composition or strength of the Spanish force. Informed by Nelson's report, Jervis sailed to intercept Córdoba on 13 February but did not confirm his location until the next day off Cape St Vincent. Only when the Mediterranean Fleet closed with Córdoba on the morning of 14 February did they learn the true size and strength of the Spanish fleet.

Fortunately for Jervis, the Spanish fleet was unprepared for battle and organized into two divisions, one to the weather and the other to the lee. Sensing the opportunity, Jervis signalled the formation of one line of battle to split Córdoba's fleet in two. The tactical plan prevented Córdoba from coordinating a defence and eliminated the opportunity for the Spanish to escape into Cádiz. Jervis turned his fleet towards the windward portion of the Spanish force as the *Excellent* and *Diadem* captured two Spanish ships of the line in rapid succession.

Nelson, disobeying Jervis' order to form a line, returned to the warship *Captain* (74 Guns) and turned his ship about to close with the enemy alone. He was quickly overwhelmed by as many as six Spanish ships, including three massive ships of the line. Capt Thomas Troubridge, commanding the *Culloden* closed the distance with the *Captain*, firing to attempt to protect Nelson's ship from the overwhelming fire from the Spanish. By 1500hrs, the *Captain* had its mainmast shot away, crippling the ship. In desperation, Nelson decided to attempt to ram the 80-gun Spanish warship *San Nicolas*. Colliding with the larger Spanish ship, Nelson and the crew of the *Captain* boarded the *San Nicolas*, forcing the crew to surrender. In one of the more bizarre incidents in maritime battles, the Spanish *San José* became entangled with the *San Nicolas* as it closed to fire on the British warship. Nelson continued his attack, leading his boarding party from the already captured *San Nicolas* onto the *San José*, capturing his second ship in the afternoon. Much of the mythology around Nelson started from this battle. His aggressiveness in action, arguably disobedient to Jervis' wishes, created instant celebrity at home. However, the battle was a success due to the teamwork and coordinated efforts of the fleet, particularly the rear division, and the actions of Collingwood and Troubridge to complete the victory.

The outcome of the battle proved a turning point in the Mediterranean for the British. The victory established a dominant position over the Spanish. Jervis captured four ships of the line at St Vincent, including the massive 114-gun *San José* and the 112-gun *Salvador del Mundo*. Córdoba retreated into Cádiz,

Nelson's boarding party used the captured *San Nicolas* as a bridge to capture the *San José* in one of the iconic stories of the admiral's career, an event retold across the Royal Navy and the British public for its ingenuity and aggressiveness. The 74-gun *Captain*, which fought much of the Battle of Cape St Vincent alone against as many as six Spanish ships, was heavily damaged in the fighting and needed two years' of repairs before it could return to service. (ARTGEN / Alamy)

where Jervis, soon to be ennobled Earl St Vincent, assumed a blockading position for much of the next four years. Córdoba proved unwilling to risk his fleet to force his way out of Cádiz, providing Jervis the freedom of action in other portions of the Mediterranean. The separation of Spanish and French forces provided an opportunity for the Mediterranean Fleet to pursue Napoleon to Egypt the next year.

Blockade of Cádiz

Following the battle of Cape St Vincent, Jervis anchored at the mouth of the Tagus in Portugal. The *Victory* and other damaged fleets returned to England. The fleet then received reinforcements, including the massive *Ville de Paris* to serve as Jervis' flagship. After the battle of Cape St Vincent, the Admiralty directed the admiral to pursue the Spanish fleet and blockade it in Cádiz. The Admiralty lacked a clear understanding of the battle, believing the Spanish fleet to be more crippled than it was, leaving Cádiz exposed to a British amphibious assault. On 31 March, Jervis led his fleet out of the Tagus estuary to attempt to force Córdoba to fight. Fighting offshore batteries and Spanish gunboats, he attempted to goad the Spanish into a battle. The station of the Mediterranean Fleet was so close to the Spanish fortifications that Nelson and a group of gunboats and the bomb vessel *Thunder* engaged in a battle with Spanish boats in the harbour, a sea battle in miniature. Efforts on 3 July and 8 July led to the loss of gunboats on both sides, but an inconclusive struggle with no indication that the newly appointed Adm José de Mazarredo would risk running the blockade with the fleet. Despite the efforts, attempts to damage Spanish gun emplacements or the fleet proved a failure. Jervis returned to Portugal in the autumn, leaving a covering squadron to maintain the blockade of Cádiz.

Jervis initially established a blockade of the port, a maritime siege that would last until the Peace of Amiens in 1802. Frigates were positioned at the mouth of the harbour to intercept any smaller vessels or maritime trade. A squadron commanded by R/Adm Thomas Louis stationed itself 15 miles offshore. Jervis positioned the rest of the fleet off Cape St Mary to respond to attempts by the Spanish to escape or any relief force arriving from other Spanish military ports or Toulon. A portion of the fleet would fall into the monotony of blockade duty outside of Cádiz. In a period of relative truce between the two sides, British captains would conduct trade with the Spanish port, often receiving traders at night. Laundry for the British fleet was even sneaked into the city, commanders often conducting these activities at night to avoid the ire of the sailors tasked with the tedious activities of anchoring outside an enemy port.

Santa Cruz

St Vincent's expedition to the Canary Islands during the blockade highlights the overly aggressive nature of the Mediterranean Fleet and the relentless pursuit of prize money. Intelligence indicated that a Spanish treasure ship *Principe de Asturias* arrived in Santa Cruz de Tenerife, carrying over seven million pounds in gold. Capturing the ship would deliver a significant blow to the Spanish treasury if successful. In April, reconnaissance from two frigates indicated that a Franco-Spanish force may also be harboured at Santa Cruz. In the midst of the 1797 mutinies, the lure of prize money also offered a way to sate frustration over the uneventful blockade of the Spanish. Jervis pounced on the opportunity. On 15 July 1797, Nelson led a squadron of three ships of the line and three frigates to Santa Cruz. Almost immediately, the expedition started unravelling. Currents and weather prevented an immediate landing. Intelligence proved wrong and the Spanish garrison possessed a much stronger defence than anticipated. On 22 July, Nelson tried again, but the lack of gunboats and only one mortar with his squadron prevented a bombardment of the defences, forcing the assault force to attack without artillery.

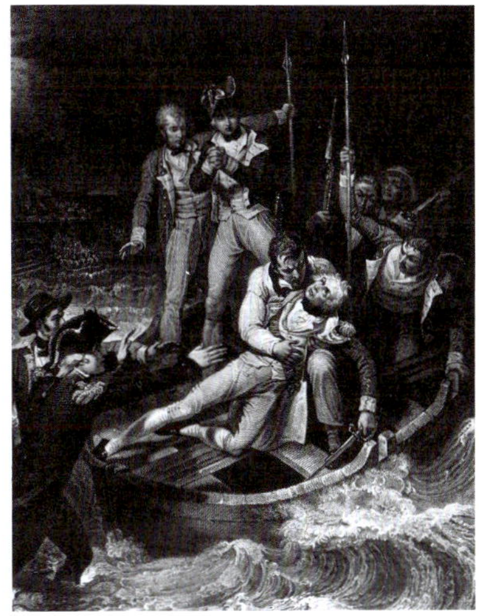

The fighting around Santa Cruz was a fiasco for Nelson and the Mediterranean Fleet. The Spanish defenders, warned of the British squadron, mobilized the inhabitants of the island to bolster the small garrison. Nelson made attacks into the strength of the Spanish defence, attempting to overcome a wild imbalance of forces with audacity. In the foolhardy attack, Nelson lost his arm and almost 700 casualties. (Hutton Archive / Getty Images)

Thwarted by his indirect assault, Nelson rashly decided to attack the main defensive position, a castle overwatching the harbour, on the night of 24 July. The Spanish defenders defeated the piecemeal attack. Unknown to Nelson and his captains, the landing force of 700 British troops assaulted into the defences of over 8,000 Spanish troops and mobilized citizens. Some of the boats landed and British attackers spiked the guns of shore batteries, but the attack was disorganized and poorly supported from the squadron. Nelson was wounded in the right arm. His surgeon on the *Theseus* amputated that night, pitching the severed limb into the harbour.

HAND-TO-HAND FIGHTING AT CÁDIZ (overleaf)

During the blockade, Jervis ordered the in-close squadron to attempt to clear the harbour of Cádiz of launches and mortar boats protecting the Spanish fleet at anchor. These types of operations reflected the dangerous nature of amphibious and ship-to-ship warfare. While marines fought with standard muskets, sailors employed in landing parties would man carronades at the bow of the boats and carry every type of weapon, from pistols and cutlasses to knives and hammers. The expeditions into Cádiz harbour were carried out under lamp light. The defences around Cádiz were formidable. In addition to the garrison and the Spanish fleet at anchor, the batteries consisted of over 80 pieces of artillery. On 3 July, Nelson led a desperate late-night attack against the screen of Spanish boats. The fighting that night was hand to hand and inconclusive. Five days later, Nelson attempted to bombard the harbour from mortar boats and an amphibious attack, but the wind prevented him from achieving any results. For the population of Cádiz, Mazarredo's defence in July 1797 was a triumph and led to a ditty about the victory: *"¿De qué sirve a los ingleses tener fragatas ligeras si saben que Mazarredo tiene lanchas cañoneras?"* (*What good is it for the English to have light frigates if they know that Mazarredo has gunboats?*) Unable to dislodge Gravina and Mazarredo from Cádiz, portions of the Mediterranean Fleet would remain on blockade of the port for the next three years, a huge demand on forces needed across the entire region with Napoleon's expedition to Egypt the following year.

The counterattack: battle of the Nile, Malta and Minorca

By 1798, the strategic situation favoured the French in the Mediterranean. While British naval power remained in control of the English Channel, Northern European waters and the Atlantic, French naval power in Toulon and military successes in Italy created opportunities for the French to expand operations in the Eastern Mediterranean. In May 1798, the French government consolidated a massive force at Toulon. Over 20,000 veteran troops marched into the naval city. Awaiting to transport this force was an armada of 30 warships, 30 brigs and over 250 support vessels. At the head of this force was Napoleon Bonaparte, fresh from his victories in the Italian campaign and successful in his ability to influence the Directory to support his plans to invade the Middle East. Napoleon's original destination was an invasion of Great Britain, but as British naval power appeared dominant in the Channel, Napoleon was able to persuade his political masters of the opportunity to strike at British possessions in India. A successful invasion could establish a foothold in the Middle East and join French forces with the Indian princes at war with Britain. The entire expedition seemed extremely ambitious, but the situation in the Mediterranean afforded an opportunity for the Directory to take a chance on the scheme.

Nelson, made aware of the French military force and the convoy out of Civitavecchia by British agents in Leghorn, sailed back into the Mediterranean, desperate to bring the French forces to battle. However, a spring squall damaged his squadron, forcing him to delay his investigation of French intentions. This delay allowed Bonaparte's flotilla to sail from Toulon on 19 May. By 31 May, this force linked up with even more ships from Corsica and other French controlled ports. By the time it arrived in Malta, the force had swelled to 36,000 troops. The Toulon fleet, under the command of V/Adm François-Paul

BATTLE OF THE NILE, 1–2 AUGUST 1798

The battle opened at about 1830hrs when the van of Nelson's fleet, with *Goliath* in the lead, crossed the face of *Guerrier* and passed between the French fort at Aboukir and the French line.

As many of Brueys' sailors were ashore and the admiral did not expect an attack from the shore, most of the port guns in the fleet were not manned or prepared for action, allowing Nelson's van to rake Brueys' fleet in the early minutes of the fighting unmolested.

By 1840hrs, the battle was joined by the centre of Nelson's force, as the *Minotaur*, *Vanguard* and *Defence* anchored along the starboard side of the French line. Every ship north of *L'Orient* was now taking fire from both sides as British crossfire began to take its toll on the majority of Brueys' fleet.

Over the next three hours, the British systematically attrited the French van. By 2100hrs, Brueys' flagship, *L'Orient*, was on fire after battling three British ships. Two other French warships drifted aground to escape the burning ship.

Only two French ships of the line escaped the battle. Just three of the nine captured French ships ever sailed again due to the extensive damage inflicted by Nelson's manoeuvre.

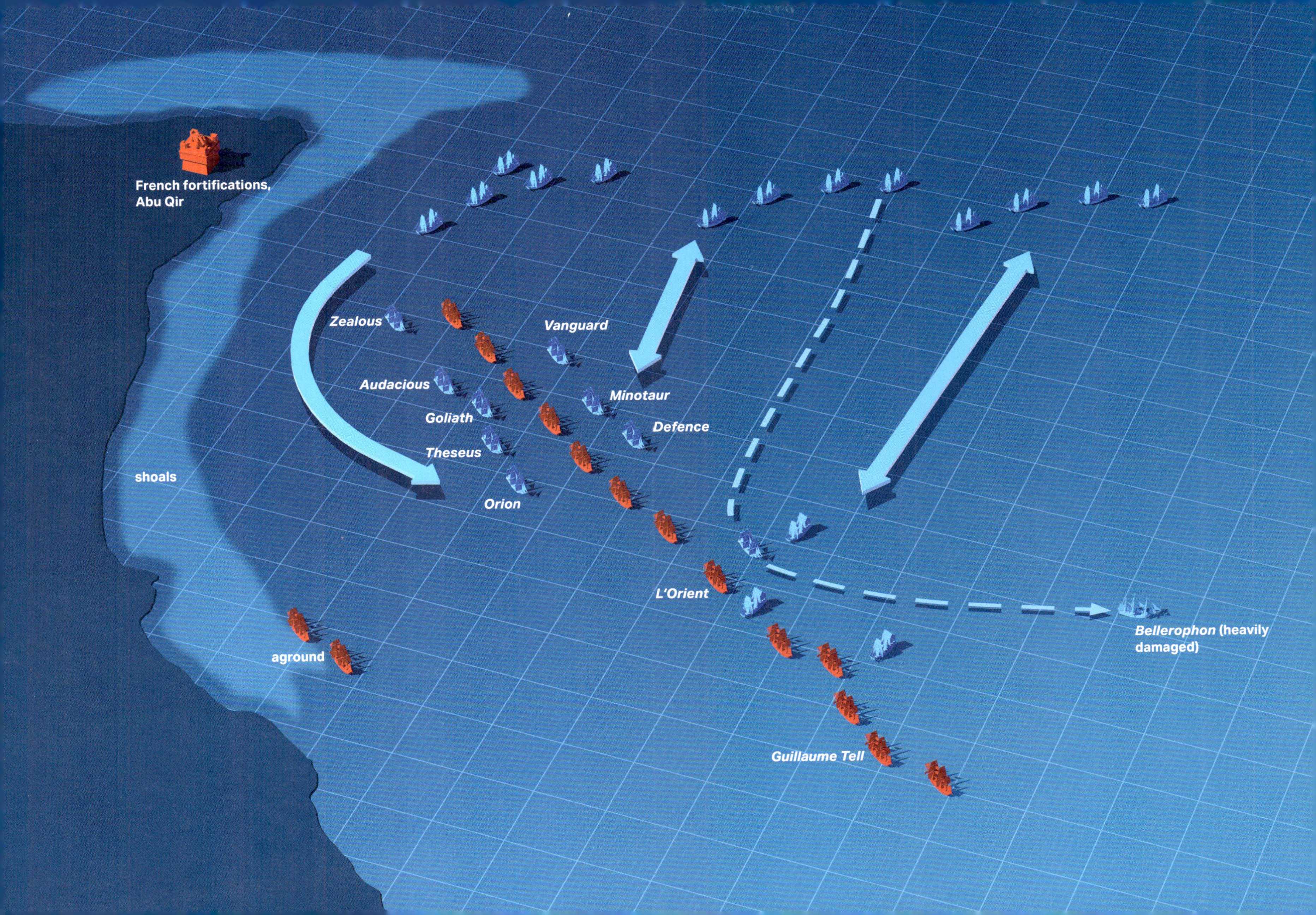
French fortifications,
Abu Qir
shoals
Zealous
Vanguard
Audacious
Minotaur
Goliath
Defence
Theseus
Orion
L'Orient
aground
Bellerophon (heavily
damaged)
Guillaume Tell

Brueys d'Aigalliers, sailed on 19 May and captured Malta in mid-June from the Knights of St John. By early June, Nelson was back in the Mediterranean with a reinforced squadron, dispatched by Jervis to confirm reports of the French fleet at sea.

The French fleet's first objective was victualling and watering the ships in Malta. Baron Ferdinand von Hompesch refused to allow the fleet to enter the harbour of Valletta, offering to permit only a few ships inside the road at a time. Napoleon responded by opening fire on the Hospitaller defenders. Many of the Knights of Malta were French; the order was feudal and badly armed. After three days of fighting, Napoleon's troops entered the city on 12 June. Bonaparte seized the gold and silver in the Catholic churches on the island, installed a republican constitution, and drafted many of the younger defenders into the French army. The French commander also released thousands of Muslim slaves, writing to the Barbary States to communicate his intentions to smooth tensions between France, Malta and the piratical states in North Africa.

By 19 June, the French force was at sea again. Bonaparte communicated his intentions to sail for Alexandria. His objectives for landing in Egypt included the liberation of the Muslim population from the Mameluks and the establishment of a launch point for military operations into the Levant. Broader strategic objectives included the capture of Ottoman territory, as Bonaparte and Charles-Maurice de Tallyrand-Périgord believed that the Ottoman Sultanate was on the verge of collapse. Both believed that Great Britain or Russia would quickly move to fill the vacuum if France did not intervene. These opinions were in contrast with many French political leaders of the early Republic, who consistently wooed the Ottoman Empire as a counterbalance to Austrian aggression. French colonialism, a political poison in the early years of French Republicanism, was on the rise in the French legislature with the waning British naval power in the Mediterranean. The French government and its dashing general were a mess of political incongruencies, exploring options for a French colony in Egypt based on Republican ideas with no slaves, an inexplicable idea born in Italian satellite republics and the disastrous revolt in the French colony of Haiti.

The battle of the Nile proved unique for battles in the Age of Sail. First, Brueys made no attempt to manoeuvre, relying on his confidence in the security of Aboukir Bay to protect the fleet. Nelson committed to an ingenious decision to split his force, risking the shoals in the harbour to pass ships between Brueys and the shore. Another rarity is that the battle began in the evening and was fought late into the night. Nelson directed markings and lighting on ships in fleet to ensure they could be identified in the dark. (DeAgostini / Getty Images)

The pursuit of the French fleet fumbled awkwardly into the Eastern Mediterranean. Nelson, back at sea and desperate to catch up, completely bypassed the French invasion of Malta. He was unaware of Bonaparte's desire to capture the island and sailed for Egypt ahead of the French force. Believing that Bonaparte intended to land in Alexandria, he arrived on 29 June. The Egyptian garrison refused access to the British squadron. Not finding the

French fleet, Nelson decided to sail for the Levant, concerned about the French landing in Syria or Alexandretta. On 1 July, two days after Nelson departed for the Levantine coast, the massive French fleet arrived in Alexandria. Nelson blamed the confusion on his lack of frigates, separated off Corsica in June before the pursuit. On 2 July, Napoleon landed with his army in Aboukir Bay to begin the invasion of Egypt. Brueys assumed a line of battle in Aboukir Bay, and anchorage where he intended to support Bonaparte's invasion force while defending himself from discovery by any pursuing British squadrons.

Finally, Nelson discovered the French fleet at Aboukir on 1 August. Brueys made serious blunders in his preparation for the battle, as his fleet was focused on protecting the anchorage, not fighting an engagement against the British. Many of his sailors from the ships of the line were ashore assisting with logistics operations for the army. Brueys also believed that Nelson would not risk a night

L'Orient was the flagship of the French fleet anchored in Aboukir Bay under the command of Brueys. The massive ship, carrying 118 guns, changed names several times during the Revolution to reflect the charged nature of domestic politics. Launched as the *Dauphin Royale*, it was renamed *Sans-Culotte* during the Jacobin era, then *L'Orient* prior to sailing for Egypt. The *Bellerophon* found itself side-by-side with *L'Orient* during the battle of the Nile and was heavily damaged by the French warship. However, repeated engagements with British ships finally caught the massive ship on fire. The French warship exploded just before midnight. As with many of Brueys' ships, it was fought undermanned due to many of its sailors being on shore as Nelson attacked. Brueys died onboard the *L'Orient* three hours before the ship exploded. (Universal History Archive / Getty Images)

BATTLE OF THE LEVANT CONVOY (overleaf)

On 7 October 1795, a French squadron of Cdre Joseph de Richery surprised the Levant Convoy off Cape St Vincent. The British force protecting the convoy was caught unprepared for Richery's force that escaped Hotham's blockade of Toulon earlier in the fall. In the battle, the *Censeur*, damaged months before and scheduled for major repairs in a home port, could not defend itself and was overwhelmed by the French line of battle. Thirty merchant ships from the convoy were also captured, the greatest defeat on a British merchant convoy in the Mediterranean since Lagos in 1693. The defeat of the convoy was one of the dark days for the Royal Navy in the Mediterranean and reflected the degradation of maritime security across the region. In British hands for less than six months, the *Censeur* was renamed *Révolution* and served in the French navy until 1799. Transferred to the Spanish, the ship was subsequently broken up. Richery's victory reflected the dangerous circumstances regarding the withdrawal of Spain from the First Coalition, a geopolitical condition that declined further when Spain allied with France in 1796.

engagement. The French admiral believed his fleet was postured close enough inshore to force the British to fight them head-on. In a brilliant manoeuvre, a portion of the British fleet split the French and sailed between the anchorage and the shore, risking running aground to encircle Brueys. Nelson, his split force on either side of Brueys, delivered a crossfire that raked a large portion of the French fleet. On this decisive day, the British sank two ships of the line, including *L'Orient* that exploded at anchor, captured nine other ships of the line, and sank two of the four frigates.

The victory in the battle of the Nile defeated Bonaparte's plan in the Levant. While Napoleon's invasion continued into the interior of Egypt, control of the Eastern Mediterranean allowed Ottoman and Russian naval power to intervene. Against the backdrop of the invasion and Nelson's victory at the Nile, diplomats were building the Second Coalition, comprising Austria, Russia, the Ottoman Empire, Naples and Great Britain. By the end of 1798, the British held strong positions across the Mediterranean and the diplomatic backing to begin mobilizing the Mediterranean for war again. Jervis unleashed his reinforced fleet across the region to begin supporting British and coalition objectives. The resurgence of British naval power, with Spanish warships contained and the Toulon fleet mangled after the Nile, was stark. Squadrons blockaded Cádiz, supported the Neapolitans off Palermo against a French invasion, and shadowed the French army advancing in the Levant. Expeditions to capture Minorca and Malta were also assembled. Joint Anglo-Russian expeditions expelled French garrisons from the Ionian Islands and threatened French positions in Italy. Together, these alliances ensured that the Mediterranean did not become a French-controlled lake and shifted the balance of power at sea firmly in Britain's favour.

Napoleon in Egypt and the Levant

While Great Britain and the European powers began to construct another coalition, the invasion of Egypt and the Levant continued. The siege of Acre (March–May 1799) represented the extent of Napoleon's invasion. After his victories in Egypt and Syria, including the brutal capture of Jaffa along the Mediterranean coast, Napoleon aimed to capture Acre, a fortified Ottoman port city, as a base for further expansion into the Levant and possibly towards India. He brought a French force of about 13,000 men, but the city's fortifications, reinforced by British naval support under Cdre Sir Sidney Smith, proved far more resilient than expected. Smith's squadron intercepted French siege artillery transported by sea and turned them over to the Ottomans to strengthen Acre's defences, leaving Napoleon without the heavy guns needed for a rapid assault.

The defenders of Acre, commanded by the Ottoman governor Jazzar Pasha and supported by Smith, mounted a determined resistance. The British fleet's bombardment prevented French approaches from the sea, while Ottoman troops repelled the repeated French assaults on the landward walls. Napoleon attempted no fewer than eight assaults between March and May 1799, but each was bloodily repulsed. Meanwhile, Ottoman reinforcements and local levies harassed the French, and disease – including plague – ravaged Napoleon's army, further sapping its strength.

By May 1799, with his army weakened and his siege lines collapsing, Napoleon abandoned the effort and retreated back towards Egypt. The failure at Acre not only ended his ambitions in the Levant but also marked the first major check to his reputation of invincibility. The British and Ottomans framed the defence as a triumph of coalition resistance, while Napoleon downplayed the setback in his reports. Strategically, the siege demonstrated the growing importance of British naval power in the Eastern Mediterranean, as well as the Ottoman Empire's capacity to resist French expansion when bolstered by European allies. It was a pivotal moment that ensured Napoleon's eastern expedition would remain a defensive struggle, not a springboard for greater imperial designs. On 22 August 1799, Napoleon abandoned his army in Egypt and slipped back into France to put plans in place to assume First Consul of the Directory.

Siege of Malta

The destruction of the French fleet at the battle of the Nile isolated the French garrison of 3,000 troops under the command of Claude-Henri Belgrand de Vaubois at Malta. On 2 September 1798, the Maltese population rose up in revolt against the French occupiers. 10,000 partisans, supported by batteries of small artillery pieces and gunboats, drove Vaubois' force into the fortifications of Valletta and the outlying island of Gozo. While the Maltese force gained control of the island, they lacked the strength to storm the robust defences around Valletta. As a part of Portugal's commitment to the Second Coalition, a small squadron of Portuguese warships sailed to the Eastern Mediterranean to join Nelson's force. After the battle of the Nile, Nelson lacked a need of the Portuguese contingent and sent the squadron back to invest Malta. James Saumarez escorted a squadron back to Gibraltar to make repairs on the ships damaged at the Nile. He could not join the siege, but on 25 September attempted to force Vaubois to surrender, which was refused. Saumarez provided supplies and muskets to the Maltese partisans and continued to Gibraltar. Until mid-October, only the Anglo-Portuguese force remained off Malta to help the revolt. During the efforts to tighten the blockade, Vaubois improved his defences with three captured Maltese warships and the arrival of the *Guillaume Tell* and two French frigates, under the command of the ill-fated Pierre-Charles Villeneuve.

The *Bellerophon* of the Arrogant class is probably one of the most famous 74s of the Revolutionary and Napoleonic Wars. It sustained damage fighting alongside the massive French ship *L'Orient* at the Battle of the Nile. Repaired, it fought in Nelson's fleet at Trafalgar and lost its captain in the fighting. Following the battle, the ship escorted the admiral's body back to England after his death. It received Napoleon's surrender after Waterloo and served as a prison ship after 1815. (FM Archive / Alamy)

For the next two years, fighting in the Mediterranean swirled around the siege of Malta. Jervis' official investment of Valletta began in October when Alexander Ball with the *Culloden*, *Colossus* and *Alexander* arrived off Malta to join the Anglo-Portuguese force. Problems quickly mounted for Ball serving as the commander of the siege. Malta was unable to feed its population by itself. The siege and political turmoil on the island threatened the native population with starvation. They also lacked the necessary resources to maintain the landward blockade around Valletta. The Neapolitan king, Ferdinand II, claimed sovereignty over the island, but lacked the desire or resources to sustain the Maltese population. The situation required Ball to requisition supplies from his own fleet and from Italy to keep the island alive.

In many ways, Ball fought his own allies and his government as much as he fought the French garrison. The success of Jervis and Nelson in 1798 was already stretching available resources. Priorities for the British Army regiments available in the region included the defence of the newly captured Minorca, maintaining pressure on Spain, concerns on the war in Italy, and the reconquering of Naples from the French. Ball requested support from the Neapolitans repeatedly without success. A cruising Russian squadron stopped briefly to join the siege but was pulled away to support the operations in the Ionian Islands in the Eastern Mediterranean. Without additional resources, Ball struggled to resist the flow of supplies into Valletta. Smaller vessels from Toulon continued to attempt to run the blockade, with schooners and a frigate evading British warships to enter the harbour.

In 1799, the French acted first. Alarm went up across the Mediterranean Fleet when V/Adm Étienne Eustache Bruix, commander of the French Atlantic fleet, evaded the Channel Fleet outside Brest and passed the straits of Gibraltar. Fears rose rapidly that this massive French force, numbering 25 ships of the line, was headed for Ireland. The Channel Fleet, losing contact with Bruix, repositioned to defend against an invasion of Ireland. However, Bruix's target was the Mediterranean, with orders to accomplish a number of critical tasks to reverse the strategic situation. First, he was ordered to relieve Malta, to reestablish the link between the two halves of the Mediterranean. Second, he was to support the ongoing operations in Corfu. Finally, he carried reinforcements and supplies for the French army in Egypt. Bruix intended to link up with Spanish forces at Ferrol but missed his rendezvous. Next, Bruix attempted to pull the Spanish fleet out of Cádiz on 4 May to join him. George Keith Elphinstone commanding the blockading squadron with 15 ships of the line, blocked his path, forcing Bruix to continue south towards Gibraltar. By 9 May, Keith abandoned the blockade of Cádiz and began the pursuit of Bruix into the Mediterranean. Nelson was forced to pull some of Ball's blockading force from Malta, temporarily lifting the siege.

At this point in early May, three different fleets were in motion in the Western Mediterranean. Bruix sailed for Toulon, arriving on 13 May. Keith's squadron, now under the command of Jervis personally, transited from Gibraltar to Mahon to unite more warships and then pursue Bruix. On 14 May, the Spanish fleet left Cádiz and entered the Mediterranean, seeking to unite with Bruix. Faced with a dangerous choice between Bruix and the 17 Spanish warships under the command of Adm José de Mazzaredo, Jervis turned his fleet to the west to confront the Spanish and prevent their juncture with the French. Mazzaredo's plans fell apart on 17 May, when a storm struck the Spanish fleet, crippling a dozen warships. The Spanish admiral sought the refuge of Cartagena, arriving at the harbour on 20 May. Bruix went back to sea on 27 May, sailing the Ligurian coastline to reinforce the armies of André Massena and Jean Moreau, heavily pressed by the Russian and Austrian armies in northern Italy. Jervis then attempted to bottle up Bruix, shifting forces between Keith's squadron and Nelson's squadron around Palermo.

Frustrated by the inability to bring Mazzaredo or Bruix to battle, tempers flared. Keith, back in command with Jervis retiring due to ill health, ordered Nelson to find Bruix. Nelson, embroiled in the politics of Naples and in the midst of his affair with Lady Emma Hamilton, the wife of the ambassador, refused to abandon the Neapolitan royal family in the midst of an invasion of Naples by a French army. Nelson also felt slighted by the appointment of Keith to command over him. Keith, incited by Nelson's philandering and insubordination, exploded. While they quarrelled, Bruix gave them both the slip and headed for Gibraltar. Unknown to both admirals, Keith and Bruix passed each other mid-June without gaining visual contact. Uniting with Mazzaredo's force and additional warships in the unguarded Cádiz, he had over 40 ships of the line, but in recognition of the preparedness of the British squadrons alerted to his presence, he decided to return to Brest. Keith finally learned Bruix's intentions in early July, almost three weeks after the French admiral left Liguria. The British admiral attempted to catch Bruix in the Bay of Biscay, but the Franco-Spanish force gained the safety of Brest. For the energy committed by the French Directory in committing Bruix to his cruise of the Mediterranean in 1799, he accomplished very little and did not impact the strategic landscape.

However, none of these manoeuvres helped Ball's problems in capturing Valletta. Bruix's fleet forced much of the blockading force at Malta to join Nelson. French resupply ships from Toulon continued to risk the hazardous journey to bring supplies to the struggling garrison in Valletta, particularly during Bruix's cruise, where British focus shifted to countering the threat. Vaubois took drastic measures to conserve supplies, forcing over 36,000 Maltese citizens out of Valletta and making Ball find suitable sustenance and housing for the destitute population. Disease ravaged the island, making little distinction between friend and foe. Ball's Portuguese allies returned to Lisbon. In November 1799, another attempt was made to force Vaubois' surrender, but the French general again refused.

Conditions rapidly improved for the British besiegers in late 1799. A Russian squadron under the command of Adm Fyodor Fyodorovich Ushakov helped the Neapolitans, supported by British artillery, retake Naples and collapsed the short-lived French satellite republic. The return of the Neapolitan royal family to their throne freed 800 British troops from Messina to join the forces on Malta. Ferdinand IV of Naples agreed to join the blockade as well, dispatching 1,200 additional troops and Neapolitan warships. On 18 February, Nelson beat back a relief force commanded by Jean-Baptiste Perrée that intended to land 3,000 additional troops and supplies.

By late summer of 1800, Vaubois lost all options as his garrison starved. The French garrison slaughtered and ate every type of living animal in Valletta. The *Guilleaume Tell* and one of the two frigates were captured attempting to escape the blockade. Firewood was in so short of supply that one French ship was broken up for firewood for the defenders. On 4 September, Vaubois asked for terms of surrender. The off and on siege of Valletta lasted over two years. 20,000 Maltese inhabitants died, mostly of disease. British terms were absolute. The island and its military stores were turned over to British control, rejecting claims by a number of interested parties, including the Russians and Neapolitans. Malta assumed a dominating point in the middle of the Mediterranean and a launch point for the British invasion of French-held Egypt the next year.

Minorca

The battle of the Nile provided the impetus to reestablish a permanent British base in the Western Mediterranean. Port Mahon on Minorca offered a well-known base to the British with modern facilities for maintaining the fleet, storehouses and a hospital. It was an exposed base attacked by the Spanish and French in previous wars. Jervis assessed the seizure of Port Mahon worth the risk. An expedition led by Charles Stuart and John Duckworth launched on 19 October 1798 to capture the island, with 6,000 troops and 20 warships.

On 7 November, Charles Stuart landed at Addya Creek on the north side of the island. As on Corsica, British naval power allowed amphibious forces to land at a time and location to surprise the enemy. Over the next few days, Stuart's small force overran Spanish batteries, driving defenders inland toward Mahon. On 9 November, Col Henry Paget, the future Earl of Uxbridge, led 300 men to storm Fort Charles at the mouth of the harbour. The capture of this position forced the collapse of Spanish resistance and allowed Duckworth's force to enter the harbour. On 11 November, a small Spanish squadron from the mainland attempted to intervene, but Duckworth's squadron easily defeated

DUCKWORTH'S CAPTURE OF MINORCA: 19 OCTOBER–16 NOVEMBER 1798

Chronology
7 November: After a brief engagement at Addaya, Spanish forces withdraw from Fournella and Addaya to Mercadel at the high point of the island.
11–14 November: Duckworth gets report of a Spanish squadron between Menorca and Mallorca. HMS Peterel is captured on 12 November and recaptured on 13 November.
14–16 November: Charles Stuart invests Ciutadella and remaining Spanish garrison. Island surrenders on 16 November; 4,000 Spanish troops, military stores, and seven merchant ships fall into British hands.
9 November: 300-man detachment under Colonel Paget marches for Port Mahon. This force captures Fort Charles at the mouth of the harbour and raises chain, allowing Aurora and Cormorant to enter Mahon.
Leviathan 74
Centaur 74
Argo 44
Dolphin 44
Aurora 28
Cormorant 20
Peterel 16
2 Armed Transports
Cutter
Merchant Transports
4,000 troops
Duckworth's Pursuit
Spanish Frigate Squadron
Ciutadella
Stuart
Mercadal
Fournella
Addaya
Paget
Port Mahon

their effort. Stuart continued to pursue the remnants of the Spanish garrison to the western end of the island, surrounding the governor and the remaining forces at Ciutadella. On 16 November, the 4,000 Spanish troops surrendered. Duckworth also seized four Spanish frigates. Stuart assumed the governorship of the island and Jervis oriented the British squadron stationed at Mahon to applying pressure on Spanish and French ports.

Battle of Algeciras

Before the Royal Navy could land troops in Egypt to eject French forces, orders were dispatched by the French Consulate for a squadron from the Atlantic ports to sail for Egypt to unite with reserve warships from the Spanish government at Cádiz. The squadron never arrived off Egypt, forced to retreat to the safety of Toulon. In June 1801, *Contre-Amiral* Charles Linois tried again to unite with the Spanish squadron in Cádiz. However, on arrival near Gibraltar, Linois learned from Cochrane, who he captured aboard his brig, the HMS *Speedy*, that Sir James Saumarez waited off Gibraltar for him with seven ships of the line. Outnumbered, Linois fell back to Algeciras Bay under the cover of Spanish batteries.

On learning of Linois' location, Saumarez decided to concentrate his squadron for battle. He sent a directive for Capt Richard Keats, blockading the mouth of the Guadalquivir River, to join him. However, Keats never closed with Saumarez's squadron, hearing contradictory information that Linois had escaped. He never participated in the first battle of Algeciras. Meanwhile, Linois lay in wait for Saumarez in Algeciras Bay, arraying his forces in a line of battle across the bay, supported by the shore batteries. The location was interesting in that it lay within visible distance of Gibraltar. Spectators from both sides flocked to the shoreline to watch the battle.

The first battle on 6 July turned into a fiasco. Becalmed winds disorganized the British attack. The *Hannibal* ran aground at the north end of the British line. As the battle progressed, *Hannibal* fought the *Formidable* and the Spanish batteries alone. Linois attempted to sever cables and move closer inland, but two

FIRST BATTLE OF ALGECIRAS: 6 JULY 1801

Saumarez decided to attempt to bring Linois' squadron to battle in Algeciras Bay, east of Gibraltar, on 5 July. On the morning of 6 July, the British squadron found Linois anchored in the bay in strong defensive positions, supported by Spanish gunboats and shore batteries.

In the five-hour battle, the attack into the teeth of defence failed. A lack of wind arrested Saumarez's squadron in range of Spanish and French fire. *Pompée* and *Hannibal* were badly damaged. Saumarez attempted to launch marines to seize the fortifications on Isla Verde, but the crippling of the *Hannibal* shifted efforts to extract the damaged warships.

Boats from the other ships were able to tow the *Pompée* out of the range of Spanish gunboats and French warships, but could not recover the *Hannibal* before it was forced to surrender. Heavily engaged, Linois ran two of his ships aground outside Algeciras to avoid becoming decisively engaged.

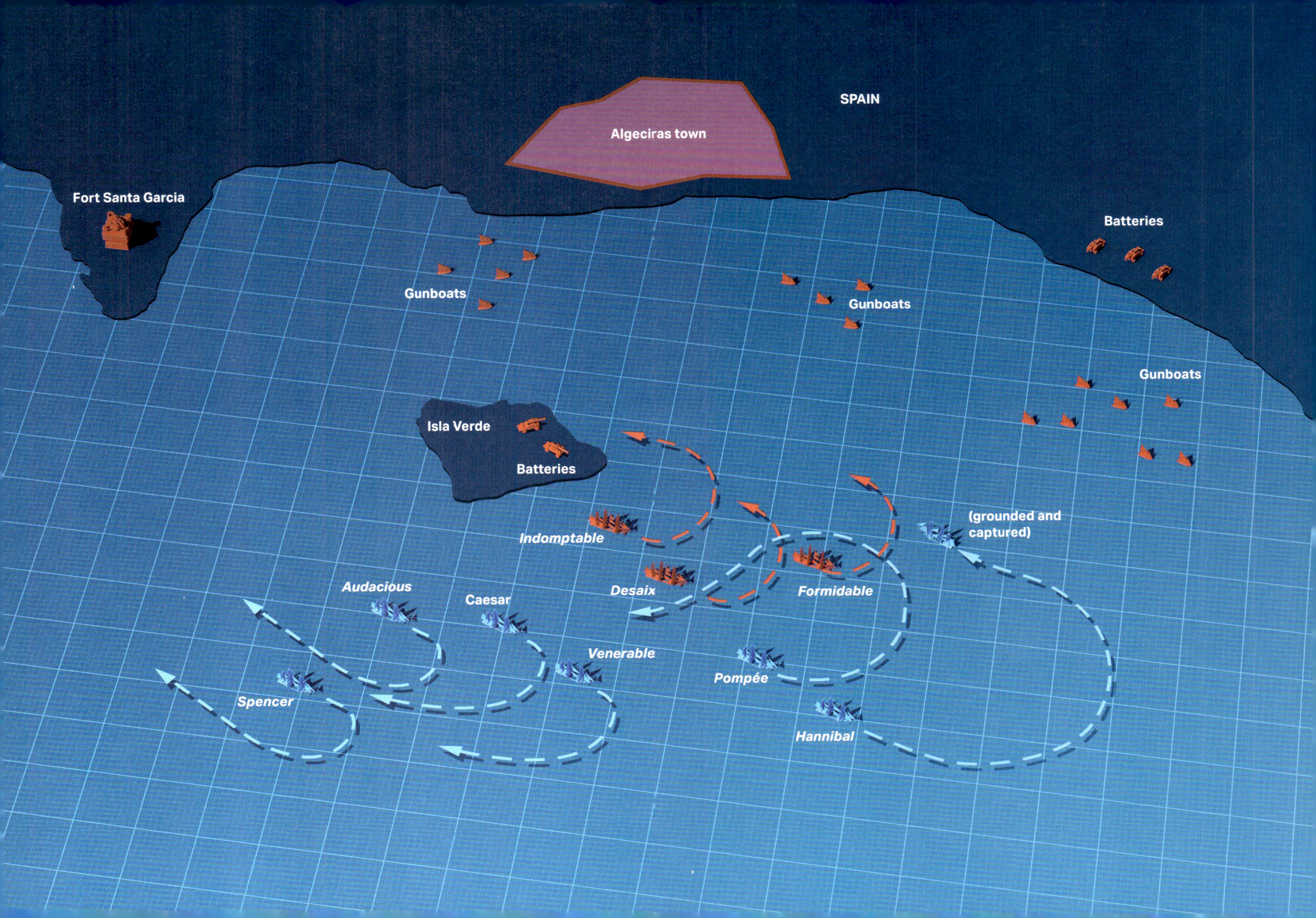
SPAIN
Algeciras town
Fort Santa Garcia
Batteries
Gunboats
Gunboats
Gunboats
Isla Verde
Batteries
(grounded and captured)
Indomptable
Audacious
Caesar
Desaix
Formidable
Venerable
Pompée
Spencer
Hannibal

The twin battles of Algeciras Bay in 1801 were fought within sight of Gibraltar. Many members of the garrison were able to watch the fighting from the port and ramparts. Because of the proximity of the British port, R/Adm James Saumarez was able to refit a portion of his squadron in less than a week. (The History Collection / Alamy)

French ships, the *Indomptable* and *Desaix* ran aground. With ships on both sides stranded, Saumarez launched boats to attempt to pull *Hannibal* out of harm's way. The batteries on Isla Verde fired on Saumarez's squadron, attempting to recover the *Hannibal* and destroy the two stranded French ships. Another British warship, HMS *Pompée*, became calmed in the inconsistent winds in the bay. French sailors evacuated the stranded ships and joined the gun crews on the island. By 1130hrs, the *Hannibal* was hopelessly stranded, grounded and lost both the main mast and mizzen mast in the hours-long duel with the Franco-Spanish defences. Saumarez launched boats again to pull the *Pompée* off the shoals, abandoning an effort to storm Isla Verde with a force of marines. By 1330hrs, the British squadron escaped Algeciras Bay, abandoning the *Hannibal*. At 1400hrs, Capt Solomon Ferris, with his ship on fire, struck the colours of the *Hannibal*.

Both sides were mauled in the inconclusive fight. French losses were over 480 sailors killed and wounded, including two captains killed in action. All three French ships of the line were heavily damaged. In addition to the loss of *Hannibal*, Saumarez's squadron suffered 472 casualties and significant damage across all vessels engaged. On 7 July, Saumarez secured the release of Ferris, his men and the crew of the *Speedy*. Ferris returned to England and a court-martial found him not guilty of negligence.

Both sides proceeded to execute rapid repairs of their ships in preparation for a renewal of hostilities. Saumarez reorganized his squadron and reassigned crews to maximize the readiness of his ships, to oppose Linois forcing the passage to Cádiz. Spanish V/Adm Juan Joachín Moreno de Mondragón arrived to reinforce Linois, planning to escort the French ships to Cádiz. As part of this strong Spanish squadron, two first rate ships, *Real Carlos* and *San Hermenegildo*, carried 112 guns apiece. The Spanish force arrived near Algeciras on 9 July, waiting outside Gibraltar battery range while Linois finished his repairs. Keats and his small force trailed Mondragón and joined forces with Saumarez in Gibraltar.

The second battle of Algeciras proved to be a great British victory and a terrible naval catastrophe. Keats, in the fastest ship in the squadron, left Saumarez with

Second battle of Algeciras. The battle was notable for British effectiveness. Saumarez made repairs to his squadron in less than a week. The battle, fought overnight on 12–13 July 1801, allowed British commanders to be aggressive. The Franco-Spanish squadron lost three ships with one captured. Saumarez's squadron suffered light casualties.

his force to pursue the Franco-Spanish squadron, which left Algeciras with a head start. Keats caught the enemy rearguard just before midnight and decided to attack on his own. In a dangerous battle in the middle of the night, the *Superb* fought all three ships: *Real Carlos*, *San Hermenegildo* and *San Antoine*. The *Superb* extinguished all of its lights, making it difficult for the Spanish and French crews to identify their target. In the confused night fighting, ships mistook their allied warships for the *Superb*, firing on each other instead of the British. One of *Superb*'s broadsides caught the *Real Carlos* on fire. The *San Antoine* surrendered. The *San Hermenegildo*, confusing the *Real Carlos* for the *Superb*, closed with the burning ship to fire broadsides. In the exchange, the *Real Carlos* crashed into the *San Hermeneglido*, the inferno passing over to the other Spanish ship. Unable to extinguish the flames, both ships exploded 45 minutes apart, killing 1,700 crewmembers in one of the greatest disasters of the war.

British invasion of Egypt

In early 1801, the British government determined the timing was right to launch an invasion to force the French army to capitulate in Egypt. Napoleon's abandonment of the army and the Ottoman pursuit after Acre forced the French back on the defensive in Egypt. They lacked supplies and support. Keith dispatched to Smith a significant force to escort the army. The squadron consisted of seven ships of the line and five frigates, and the troop transports to carry 21,000 British troops. By 8 March, the landing force of 5,200 men were postured in boats to storm ashore at Aboukir into the face of a French force defending against the

'The Battle of Alexandria, 21 March 1801', Philip James de Loutherbourg (1802). The fighting in Egypt ended on 2 September 1801 when Menou surrendered the remaining French troops at Alexandria. As a part of the peace settlement, the Ottoman and British commanders split the French warships left in Alexandria harbour. The surrender also delivered Egyptian antiquities into the hands of the British, including the Rosetta Stone. French forces were repatriated on British warships. (©National Galleries of Scotland / Bridgeman Images)

landings. In a brisk assault, the landing parties gained control of the beachhead, supported by fire from Smith's squadron. By the end of 8 March, the entirety of MajGen Ralph Abercromby's army was ashore.

Over the next four months, the British steadily pushed the 13,000-man army under Jacques-François de Menou back into the defences around Alexandria. Abercromby died of wounds in one of the engagements, but Menou surrendered after a siege of the city on 2 September 1801. The British repatriated 10,000 French troops to France, but seized the military stores, cannons and warships of Menou's force. The expedition had been a triumph for British amphibious cooperation and secured holdings across the region, but it did not bring the war to an end. Both sides continued to struggle throughout 1801 without creating conditions for a victory.

Sidney Smith and The Defence of Acre

Napoleon's siege of Acre shone a light on one of Britain's most flamboyant commanders at the climax of the Levant invasion. Napoleon's *Armée d'Orient* held designs for the capture of Jerusalem after it seized the fortifications at Acre, defended by Jazzar Pasha and his Ottoman garrison. Napoleon invested the coastal city on 20 March 1799 with only infantry, expecting Ottoman resistance to collapse. When Jazzar refused to surrender, Napoleon began barging his heavy artillery along the coastline from Jaffa. Sidney Smith pounced, seizing the French barges and cutting the littoral supply line back to Egypt. As the coast road ran dangerously close to the war, Smith's gunboats accompanying the flotilla stood in close to the shore and bombarded the French columns reinforcing the siegeworks. Smith took the *Tigre* and *Theseus*, his two ships of the line, and anchored adjacent to Acre's defences. The two warships cannonaded the French lines. Smith also transferred the captured French guns to the Ottomans for the defence of the city.

The two-month siege outside Acre broke Napoleon's army. While the French general brought additional siege guns from more inland routes, the British and Ottoman defenders built an additional wall to the interior of the main defensive works. When Napoleon's artillerymen finally breached the outer wall of the defences and conducted their assault on 10 May, they found another formidable wall that would take time to breach. With the outbreak of plague and significant casualties from the incessant artillery, Napoleon recognized he could not keep his army in such an exposed position. With local dominance of the sea, the British blockade of possible resupply ports along the route from Egypt to the Levant helped to make Napoleon's position in front of Acre untenable.

'Defence at the breach of St Jean d'Acre, 8 May 1799', Thomas Sutherland (1815). Sidney Smith not only brought cannons to the Ottoman defenders at Acre but also contributed sailors and marines to the defence. Antoine de Phélippeaux, a French Royalist who helped Smith escape prison in France in 1797, employed a group of labourers to improve the defences on the landward side of the fortification that stymied Napoleon's assault on 8 May. In the desperate assault, the French army was unable to capture the second wall Phélippeaux had constructed behind the breach. (Historica Graphica Collection / Heritage Images / Getty Images)

Amiens

The Peace of Amiens, signed in March 1802 between France and Britain, temporarily ended hostilities in the War of the Second Coalition and marked the first general peace in Europe since 1792. While the British gained victories across the region, taking Malta and Minorca, Keith and Smith had ejected the French from Egypt, putting the Mediterranean Fleet in its strongest position since 1793. However, the Spanish and French fleets remained a threat. Napoleon's victory at Marengo and the French victory at Hohenlinden defeated the allies in Europe. Britain recognized the French Republic and agreed to restore most of its colonial conquests, while France promised to withdraw from Naples, the Papal States and Egypt. The treaty also included provisions for the independence of the Batavian Republic and Switzerland, and for Malta to be restored to the Order of St John under the protection of a neutral power. For war-weary Europe, the agreement brought a brief respite from a decade of almost continuous conflict, though from the outset both sides viewed the peace as an interlude rather than a permanent settlement.

Despite the formal settlement, deep tensions persisted. Britain was alarmed by Napoleon's expanding influence in continental Europe, where French troops remained in the Netherlands, Switzerland and Italy, in defiance of the spirit of the treaty. At the same time, France grew suspicious of Britain's dominance at sea and its retention of several key colonies, such as Trinidad and Ceylon, which had been captured during the war. Napoleon's continued reorganization of Europe's political landscape – particularly his interventions in Switzerland and Italy – heightened British fears that France sought outright hegemony, undermining the fragile trust required for the treaty to hold.

The Mediterranean quickly became one of the most contentious flashpoints. Central to this was the issue of Malta, a strategically vital naval base controlling access between the Eastern and Western Mediterranean. Under the terms of the treaty, Britain was supposed to evacuate Malta once the Knights of St John had been restored and its independence guaranteed. Yet Britain delayed the evacuation, citing concerns about France's growing naval presence in Toulon and its ambitions in the region. Napoleon, for his part, viewed Britain's refusal to leave Malta as a blatant violation of the treaty. The struggle over Malta symbolized the broader strategic rivalry: Britain was determined to maintain maritime supremacy, while France sought influence in the Mediterranean as a springboard for its ambitions in the Levant and beyond.

By 1803, the peace collapsed entirely. The immediate cause was the dispute over Malta, but the underlying reasons ran deeper: irreconcilable differences between Britain's global, naval-oriented empire and Napoleon's expansionist Continental System. Both sides had signed the Peace of Amiens not out of genuine reconciliation but as a tactical pause to regroup. Britain, financially strong but militarily overstretched, needed time to consolidate its naval and colonial gains, while France sought to secure the Continent and stabilize its revolutionary regime. Once it became clear that neither side would yield in the Mediterranean or in Europe, war resumed in May 1803, inaugurating a new phase of the Napoleonic Wars.

The path to Trafalgar

Britain declared war on France in May 1803; the strategic situation had turned in favour of the French. The Royal Navy only had 83 ships of the line available after economizing during the tenuous peace. Napoleon continued to make preparations for an invasion from Boulogne across the Channel to England. The blockade of Brest was of vital importance to the British war plan. In the Mediterranean, immediate concern was the control of the central portion of the Mediterranean. Protection of Sicily and Malta to maintain the alliance and strategic gateways was critical. The British government was immediately concerned about a repeated French adventure to the Levant and the fears of the Toulon fleet transiting to Brest. Nelson also needed to commit warships to monitor activities in Toulon. To accomplish both, the Mediterranean Fleet was stationed at the Maddalena Islands off the northern tip of Sardinia. The Spanish declaration of war in 1804 only made Nelson's position more tenuous.

The Napoleonic obsession with invading England was driving French naval plans. The First Consul had amassed 165,000 troops at Boulogne by July 1803, but efforts to establish a viable transport system repeatedly failed. Napoleon's trial runs resulted in the sinking of 30 transport vessels, complicated by the harsh weather, difficult harbour conditions and the growing British defensive preparations. Napoleon's problem was concentration. With the Spanish, he held a larger naval force, but it was distributed between seven French and allied ports. Napoleon developed multiple plans to affect this concentration in the Channel, but commanding navies is not like commanding armies. Much of the planning developed around false expectations that French warships could escape blockades and race to a rendezvous location. The Mediterranean war of the previous decade proved precise movements of naval forces extremely unpredictable. Napoleon's assumptions also hinged on British admirals surrendering their blockading positions along the French coastline, hence leaving the English Channel unguarded to pursue enemy squadrons. The French plans were ambitious in the extreme and failed to appreciate the fundamental realities of fighting the Royal Navy.

In January 1805, the French navy put their first attempt to control the English Channel in motion. The Rochefort squadron slipped out of port on 11 January

By 1801, the British government became increasingly concerned about the concentration of French forces in the northwest corner of France, staging grounds for a cross-Channel invasion. Napoleon's camp at Boulogne is best known, but French naval preparations at Brest caused considerable fear. Nelson made two attempts in August 1801 to destroy the French flotilla at Brest but was repulsed in both attacks. The second attack had over 2,000 sailors and marines as part of the assault party. (The Print Collector / Getty Images)

to make for the West Indies to link up with the Toulon fleet. Villeneuve, now in the command of the Toulon fleet after the death of Latouche-Tréville, left harbour three days later, slipping past Nelson's frigates to sail for Gibraltar. Within two days of Villeneuve's departure, the French plan fell apart. Napoleon cancelled the operation due to unfavourable conditions. Villeneuve ran into weather in the Mediterranean and was forced back to Toulon. Nelson, believing Villeneuve's destination was the Eastern Mediterranean, cruised the Levant looking for him, but did not learn of Villeneuve's return until mid-February.

In March, Napoleon tried again. Martinique was directed as the rally point for Villeneuve, Ganteaume, and ships from Ferrol to create a combined French fleet of significant size. Under Ganteaume's command, they would sail to the Channel. On 30 March, Villeneuve sailed from Toulon with 11 ships of the line and escaped the Mediterranean. Orde, guarding Cádiz with five ships of the line, withdrew into the Bay of Biscay to block Villeneuve, allowing a Spanish squadron under Gravina to escape the blockade and join Villeneuve. Despite being outnumbered, Orde had correctly surmised French intentions and his decision played a critical role in the outcome of the campaign. Nelson, unaware of Villeneuve's decision, did not reach Gibraltar until 6 May, a full month behind the French fleet.

The intervention of Barham and Pitt saved the campaign. On 30 April, the prime minister and Barham recognized the gravity of the situation. In April, Russia and Great Britain signed an alliance that included the commitment of a British army to the Mediterranean. This small army sailed for Malta on 19 April. Barham and Pitt realized that neither Orde nor Nelson knew this army was sailing for the Mediterranean and Villeneuve was somewhere west of Gibraltar. The risks were immense. That night, Barham directed the detachment of Collingwood with 14 ships of the line to regain control of Cádiz and the waters around Gibraltar. In typical maritime fashion, Villeneuve and the Spanish squadron at Cartagena did not know about the British army convoy or they both would have moved to destroy the slow-moving force at sea. The arrival of Collingwood and Nelson at the mouth of the Mediterranean provided enough security to ensure the convoy reached Malta and provided a strong British naval presence.

The cat-and-mouse chase between fleets spilled over into the Caribbean. Villeneuve waited off Martinique with Gravina in hopes of uniting with Ganteaume. Unknown to the allied admirals, Ganteaume never made it out of Brest, unwilling to risk his fleet attempting to force a passage through the British squadron. Napoleon dispatched fresh orders to Villeneuve, directing him to capture British colonies. Villeneuve had no intelligence on the arrival of Nelson in the Caribbean until 4 June. He then decided to sail for Europe to follow Napoleon's directives, with Nelson in pursuit.

Barham, now First Lord of the Admiralty, received a report from Nelson on Villeneuve sailing back to European waters and made his second fateful decision of the campaign. He directed the lifting of the blockade at Rochefort and sent the squadron to join Calder off Ferrol. The decision-making and communications speed from Nelson to Barham to Cornwallis was so quick that Calder consolidated his force outside Ferrol a week before the Villeneuve-Gravina force arrived from the Caribbean. The two forces clashed at Cape Finisterre on 22 July in a fog, a confusing fight resulting in Gravina losing two ships. Blocked from getting to the Channel, Villeneuve retreated to Vigo on 2 August. The continued concentration of British naval power off the Iberian coastline broke Villeneuve's will, forcing him back to Cádiz where Calder blockaded him on 21 August. Meanwhile, Napoleon waited in Boulogne, flummoxed by the supposed ineptitude of his admirals and clueless to the difficulties of naval service.

Trafalgar

As Napoleon turned his army from Boulogne on 25 August to begin the march against the Austrians, forces began converging around Cádiz. Cornwallis, commanding the Channel Fleet, detached 20 ships of the line on 15 August to sail to join the Mediterranean Fleet, taking a risk on leaving a smaller force guarding the Channel, but with confidence in the location of the Franco-Spanish fleet. Despite all of the celebration of Nelson's 'Band of Brothers', the majority of the captains at Trafalgar would command the detached Channel warships. Many of those commanders knew Nelson by reputation alone. Nelson himself sailed from England on 15 September with the *Victory* after a month of shore leave.

Nelson's plan was to lure Villeneuve out of Cádiz. Both fleets were in desperate need of supplies, but Villeneuve was initially hesitant to put his fleet at risk against the British. Napoleon, however, issued the order on 16 September for Villeneuve to sail for Naples and deliver his reinforcements to support operations in Italy. The French admiral dithered for over a month, uncertain of the risks and taking counsel from the Spanish and French officers, who urged caution. On 18 October, Villeneuve finally gave the order to sail out of Cádiz with the combined fleet.

Nelson caught the combined fleet off Cape Trafalgar on 21 October in a disorganized formation. On sighting the 27 ships of the British fleet, Villeneuve gave the order for his fleet to head back to Cádiz and ensure the security of the harbour. Nelson's plan before the battle was to attack in three columns to split the enemy fleet at multiple points, but he was also confident in British sailing skill and gunnery and was comfortable with a *melee* where ship-to-ship combat favoured the British. The combined fleet was significantly larger and the risk in giving battle was the ability for two or three enemy ships to focus fire on a British ship, as Nelson experienced on the *Captain* at Cape St Vincent eight years earlier.

At noon, the battle was joined between the two fleets. The combined fleet was arrayed in a crescent shape due to the struggles in sailing the large force and the turn Villeneuve made to return to Cádiz. Two British columns, led by the

Royal Sovereign and the *Victory,* punched a hole through the enemy fleet in 45 minutes. The general *melee* Nelson expected ensued. As Nelson lay dying below deck on the *Victory*, his fleet completely overwhelmed the centre and rear of the enemy fleet. Enemy losses included 17 ships of the line surrendered, while the *Achille* was destroyed in the battle. Many of the British prizes were wrecked in the subsequent storm following the battle. A few of the French warships in the van of Villeneuve's fleet escaped but were captured in a subsequent engagement on 4 November. A significant portion of French and Spanish naval power was devastated in an afternoon.

ANALYSIS

The combat record of the Mediterranean Fleet is not unblemished. By 1795, French victories in the Pyrenees and the Italian Alps neutralized British naval power. Two years later, the Mediterranean Fleet withdrew entirely from the region, overwhelmed by French success in Italy and the Franco-Spanish alliance. The Mediterranean Fleet was beset by manning and logistical challenges; it endured mutinies; its admirals fought amongst each other, the diplomatic corps, their political masters in London and the British Army. The fleet itself missed opportunities to destroy French forces and lost convoys to French squadrons. While it achieved success at sea, particularly during the War of the Second Coalition, naval power could not prevent French military victories in 1796 or 1800 that annihilated British alliances on the Continent. Indeed, it was the compounding effects of British victories at sea over time, not just Trafalgar, which forced Napoleon to enforce the Continental System, a European blockade of British goods.

At small actions and fleet battle, the Mediterranean Fleet proved extremely capable. The aggressiveness of individual captains and the gunnery of the fleet led commanders to assume risk in bringing the British and Spanish to battle. Where the British truly outclassed the French and Spanish was in ship-on-ship combat. Commander decisions and wind impacted the decisiveness of the battle, but at the broadside level, British tactical superiority and the cool heads of their captains outfought the enemy. The courage of a commander to bring a ship alongside the enemy and exchange raking broadsides regularly won the day. The training of gun crews proved able to overcome numbers, surprise and a list of other factors. In the confines of the Mediterranean, outside French and Spanish home ports, this level of aggressiveness paid repeated dividends in imposing physical and psychological attrition on the enemy.

Combining engagements with the pressure of blockade, the Mediterranean Fleet, day by day, eroded the confidence of Napoleon and his admirals on the efficacy of naval warfare against the British. French and Spanish fleets often proved unwilling to risk battle unless forced. The number of captured and destroyed ships weighed in the favour of the British. The ability of the

Mediterranean Fleet to block Cartagena, Cádiz and Toulon hastened the erosion of readiness across enemy fleets and crews, being unable to consistently put to sea. By 1805, the war in the Mediterranean changed dramatically in character from a contest between naval power to an effort to enforce a continental-wide blockade against Napoleonic France and its satellites. This process was not easy – as Nelson at Santa Cruz, or Saumarez at Algeciras, could attest. But the methodical erosion of French and Spanish readiness, combined with the punctuated victories at St Vincent, the Nile and Trafalgar, together with dozens of victories by frigate captains, ground down French naval power. Critical to the success of this blockade strategy was the continuous investment from the British state in the Mediterranean theatre, particularly after 1797. Logistics was diverse, but consistent. The fleet and its bases became more stable as the war with France progressed, emboldened by regular reinforcements and a commitment to providing for the ships and crews. These efforts allowed the fleet to maintain pressure on enemy ports.

Other aspects of naval warfare proved less successful; results in amphibious operations and support to allied armies were more mixed. Many of the fleet's senior officers were too ambitious, willing to take significant risks in landward attacks with flimsy knowledge of enemy strength and dispositions. Intelligence in these operations often proved inaccurate, leading to infighting between the army and navy leadership on the appropriate course of action. On Corsica, against a weak and demoralized enemy, amphibious operations proved decisive. On Santa Cruz, the amphibious landing proved a fiasco, almost leading to Nelson's death. Sidney Smith provided incredible support to the Ottomans defending Acre against Napoleon and Nelson's support to the Neapolitans in 1799. In Liguria in 1795–1796, the fleet proved totally ineffective. At Aboukir, amphibious operations triumphed. However, the commitment of the state to the region provided the senior officers in the fleet with the tools necessary to gain a decisive advantage in the region and change the parameters of the war against Napoleon.

On 8 March 1801, landing parties from the 21,000-man army under MajGen Ralph Abercromby landed in Aboukir Bay. Over the course of a few hours, the 5,200-man assault force swept aside the French defenders to begin the invasion of Egypt to eject Menou's army. The amphibious operation was so effective that the majority of the British Army was landed in one day. (©Historical Picture Archive / Corbis / Getty Images)

FURTHER READING

Baker, Casey. *Britain's War for the Mediterranean: The Fight against Revolutionary France*. Annapolis: Naval Institute Press, 2024.

Caputo, Sara. *Foreign Jack Tars: The British Navy and Transnational Seafarers during the Revolutionary and Napoleonic Wars.* Cambridge: Cambridge University Press, 2024.

Clarke, James Stanier and James McArthur. *Naval Chronicle*. 38 Volumes: 1799–1818.

Gardner, Robert, ed. *The Campaign of Trafalgar, 1803–1805*. London: Mercury, 2005.

Gardner, Robert, ed. *Fleet Battle and Blockade: The French Revolutionary War, 1793–1797*. London: Mercury, 2005.

Gregory, Desmond. *The Ungovernable Rock: A History of the Anglo-Corsican Kingdom and Its Role in Britain's Mediterranean Strategy During the Revolutionary War, 1793–1797*. London: Fairleigh Dickinson University Press, 1985.

Gregory, Desmond. *Malta, Britain, and the European Powers, 1793–1815.* London: Fairleigh Dickinson, 1996.

Gregory, Desmond. *Minorca, The Illusory Prize: A History of the British Occupations of Minorca between 1708 and 1802.* London: Fairleigh Dickinson, 1990.

Ireland, Bernard. *The Fall of Toulon*. London: Weidenfeld and Nicolson, 2005.

Knight, Roger. *The Pursuit of Victory: The Life and Achievement of Horatio Nelson*. London: Basic, 2005.

Lambert, Andrew. *Nelson: Britannia's God of War*. London: Faber, 2004.

Lavery, Brian. *Nelson's Navy: The Ships, Men, and Organisation, 1793–1815.* Annapolis: Naval Institute Press, 1989.

Le Fevre, Peter and Richard Harding. *Precursors of Nelson: British Admirals in the Eighteenth Century*. Mechanicsburg, PA: Stackpile, 2000.

Mackesy, Piers. *The War in the Mediterranean, 1803–1810*. Cambridge: Harvard University Press, 1957.

McCranie, Kevin. *Admiral Lord Keith and the Naval War against Napoleon.* Gainesville: University Press of Florida, 2006.

Meeks, Joshua. *France, Britain, and the Struggle for the Revolutionary Western Mediterranean*. London: Palgrave, 2017.

Musteen, Jason. *Nelson's Refuge: Gibraltar in the Age of Napoleon*. Annapolis: Naval Institute Press, 2011.

Pocock, Tom. *A Thirst for Glory: The Life of Admiral Sir Sidney Smith.* London: Pimlico, 1996.

Reid, Stuart. *Egypt, 1801: The End of Napoleon's Eastern Empire*. Barnsley: Frontline, 2021.

Rodger, N. A. M. *The Wooden World: An Anatomy of the Georgian Navy.* London: W. W. Norton, 1986.

Rodger, N. A. M. *The Command of the Ocean: A Naval History of Britain, 1649–1815*. New York: W. W. Norton, 2005.

INDEX

Figures in **bold** refer to photos and illustrations.